THE SECRET TO
CYBERSECURITY

A SIMPLE PLAN TO PROTECT
YOUR FAMILY AND BUSINESS
FROM CYBERCRIME

SCOTT E. AUGENBAUM

www.scotteaugenbaum.com

Published by Forefront Books.

Cover Design by Bruce Gore, Gore Studio Inc.
Interior Design by Bill Kersey, KerseyGraphics

ISBN: 978-1-948-67708-0 print
ISBN: 978-1-948-67709-7 e-book

HERO
PUBLISHING

ACKNOWLEDGMENTS

IF YOU WOULD HAVE TOLD ME MORE THAN THIRTY YEARS ago that I would be enjoying retirement after an amazing career with the Federal Bureau of Investigation, married to the woman of my dreams, and the author of a book about cybersecurity, I would have told you that's not my life. As I look back on this journey, I am reminded that you are only as strong as the people you surround yourself with. Throughout my career, I met so many incredible people who inspired me, and I've listed a few who made this dream possible.

If it was not for my mom, Alice Augenbaum, I never would have found that entry-level job with the FBI. If she hadn't filled out the application for me, who knows where I'd be today.

My friend Natalie O'Connell pushed me to go back to college at City College in New York. She also inspired me to work on an MBA in Information Technology at Fordham University, which led to my passion for technology.

Supervisory Special Agent (SSA) Robert Grubert of the FBI's New York office was my supervisor for six years. He provided all the tools I needed to succeed. I also wouldn't have made it without the friendship and support of several special agents, including Philip Sarcione, Joseph Cervini, Robert Leneck, and the late James Downey.

While assigned to the Syracuse Resident Agency, I was mentored by four of the greatest FBI agents around: John Winslow, Philip Looney, Robert Haley, and my Supervisor Michael Mason. I had numerous great friendships with so many other awesome people while working there.

While assigned to FBI headquarters in Washington, D.C., I wouldn't have made it there for three years without the friendships of Ray Goergen, Todd Ratcliff, and Leslie Bryant.

In Nashville, I had the support and friendship of Matthew Dunn, Richard Campbell, Randy Bechtel, and Keith Moses. Together we ran the Nashville Division and made sure our staff was proud to work for the FBI. Special Agent in Charge of the Houston Division, Perrye Turner, pushed me to go back and finish my MBA, as well as continue a lifelong path of education.

I'd especially like to thank John McMurtrie, Brandon Harcum, John Medeiros, Jeff Dale, Casper Cromwell, Cameron Beall, Dean Kinsman, and Merridee Isabell for being my direct reports during my seven years as a supervisor. Thanks for making my life so easy. To Matthew Espenshade, Jeff Peterson, and Jeremy Baker, thanks for being true leaders and allowing me to do my job.

How can I not mention Victor Rodriguez, my good friend and trusted lieutenant, with his encyclopedic knowledge of technology. I'd also like to commend my friends at the Tennessee Bureau of Investigation and Franklin Police Department, such as Kevin Williams, Cesar Salazar, Richard Littlehale, Mark Gwyn, and Eric Anderson, for their uncondi- tional support to the Nashville Cyber Task Force. We couldn't have kept the community safe without you guys.

To my great friend and former FBI Agent Jason Smolanoff, Senior Managing Director, Cyber Risk: your guidance, support, and friendship allowed me to follow my passion to teach individuals and organizations how not to be the next cybercrime victim.

David Briggs of First Tennessee Bank invited me to scare his clients, which is where I met my current business partner and close friend, David Byerley. When I met David, I told him my goal was to write a book and speak around the country on keeping people safe. David convinced me I should aim much higher and instead of educating the country, why not educate the world? David provided me with the confidence to aim much higher than I could on my own.

I'd also like to thank my family at Hero Publishing for taking a retired FBI agent's dreams and using them to make the world a better and safer place. I am blessed to work with such a team of superstars: Matt Rigsby, Blake Byerley, Sam Lingo, Josh Oakes, Zak Manning, Hannah Paramore, Holly Hubert, Betsy Woundenberg, and Paul Clements. Paul is an amazing nonfiction author who took my original 70,000-word manuscript and made it into a meaningful story that flowed.

I can't forget my friends Darren Mott, Robert Bannazia, Mike Rech, Rich Hlvati, Jordon Flowers, Dan Wittig, Don Baham, Brien Welsh, Bill Mulholland, Don Slaughter, Maria Dominici, Don "Mac" McCarthy, and Wiley Robinson, who've all been tortured by me asking, "What do you think about this story or point?"

Jonathan Merkh at Forefront Books and his team made this book a reality, and I spent the past several months with Mark Schlabach working on this project and perfecting the story.

To my sister, Bonni, and brother in-law, Rick, and nieces Emily and Sydney, thanks for your love and support over the years. To my brother, Stephen, thanks for making me laugh.

Words can't describe how much I love my wife, Maureen, and appreciate her for allowing me to chase my dreams. Writing a book takes a tremendous amount of effort and patience, and she understood how important it was for me to get my story published. I have no idea where she comes up with the patience to put up with me, and because of her I am a much better person. To my boys Aidan and Quinn, thanks for keeping me young. I'm always so proud of both of you.

Finally, thank you to the brave men and women of the FBI, who day in and day out continue to keep the country safe, and to the Federal Bureau of Investigation Agents Association, which never stops fighting for their rights.

Scott E. Augenbaum
www.scotteaugenbaum.com

CONTENTS

INTRODUCTION

Fear from Real Experience

IT'S HARD TO BELIEVE THAT IT WAS FEWER THAN TWENTY-FIVE
years ago when America Online (AOL) and its "You've Got Mail!" slogan
ruled the World Wide Web. It's also hard to believe that the Internet,
which was once considered nothing more than a novelty, would bring
so many great things into our lives.

But while we've been greatly enriched by the wealth of information,
entertainment, goods, and services provided by the Internet, nobody
ever really considered how much crime would come with it. Who would
have ever imagined that plugging an Ethernet cable into the back of our
computer or connecting our laptop, cell phone, or tablet to a wireless
network in an airport would become an open door for criminals to ruin
our lives and destroy the economy?

I was one of the first special agents from the Federal Bureau of
Investigation assigned to investigating cybercrime back in the late
1990s. At the time, we were chasing amateur hackers, thrill seekers,
and teenagers who were mostly more mischievous and adventurous
than criminal.

When I joined the FBI, I never could have imagined cybercrime
would become my specialty. I was twenty years old when I was hired as
a file clerk in the FBI's New York field office in 1988. After my mother
completed the application and submitted it on my behalf, she handed
me $100 to buy two pairs of polyester slacks, four dress shirts, and two
ties. I knew very little about computers and even less about the Internet.

I eventually went back to college at night and was promoted to
start doing more accounting and financial work within the FBI. Then I
started working on an MBA in finance and information technology at
Fordham University. The best part about attending Fordham was being
surrounded by so many mentors—professors *and* the students who
openly challenged them about the concepts they taught and whether
things were being done the right way. I really enjoyed the challenge
and had a renewed sense to learn. I just didn't know if a career in law
enforcement and the FBI was the correct path for me.

I'd always been told that becoming an FBI agent was extremely difficult, and there was a hiring freeze in place, anyway. So, once I completed
my MBA at Fordham, I was pretty sure I wanted to find a job on Wall

Street. I wanted to introduce people who *needed* something to people who *had* something—and take my cut of the financial pie for making the deal happen. Even though I'd been working with the FBI for six years, I was still living in the same bedroom in my mother's house that I'd been sleeping in since I was five years old. I knew I needed to start getting on with my life.

But, before I could leave the FBI for a job on Wall Street, an unexpected opportunity opened up for me. The FBI's hiring freeze came to an end in the spring of 1994 and it started hiring new agents. People who already worked for the Bureau were given top priority, and my supervisor (who was like a father figure to me) encouraged me to apply. Much to his surprise, I told him I wasn't interested in becoming an agent. He looked disappointed and then angry. He sternly told me I *was* going to apply to become an agent.

About six months later, I left for new-agent training in Quantico, Virginia. I lost twenty pounds, passed the written test, interview, medical examination, background check, and polygraph test. When I graduated from new-agent training, I thought I'd be sent back to work in New York City or maybe even my first choice, Boston. Instead, I was assigned to a field office in Syracuse, New York. That might as well have been Iowa or Nebraska as far as I was concerned.

If you would have asked me what my job description was in June 1995, it would have been very easy to describe: *there were bad people doing bad things to good people, and my job was to work with state and local law enforcement to put the bad guys in jail.* The end goal was to make upstate New York a much safer place for everyone. I worked a lot of white-collar crime, bank robberies, stolen property, and fugitive cases in the Northern Judicial District of New York. Really, I worked anything that came through the door as a new agent and the lowest man on the totem pole. I didn't care. I had a gun, badge, and car with lights and sirens, and I was allowed to go out and play "Cops and Robbers" with my colleagues. It was a rewarding experience, and we managed to put a lot of bad people in jail.

The turning point for me occurred in 1996, when I received a call from a representative of a small Internet service provider in upstate

New York who wanted to talk about stolen property being sold over these things called *bulletin boards*. I met with the man and everything he described seemed so foreign to me. I'd taken a few programming courses in high school, and I probably knew more about computers than most FBI agents. The release of Windows 95 made things much easier for computer novices. It was almost plug-and-play for users like me, and that's how I became interested in computers. It suddenly occurred to me, though, that I needed to learn a lot more about computers, the Internet, and the growing threat of cybercrime.

I was so motivated that I went home and purchased a $2,500 Gateway computer system, which had a blazing fast 133 MHz processor and 40 MB hard drive. That probably made me the only FBI agent in my field office who owned a personal computer. I enrolled in an Internet course at the State University of New York at Oswego, but I had to cover the costs myself. My supervisor couldn't understand why the FBI needed to be concerned about what was happening on the Internet! He couldn't have known that I would retell that story thousands of times over the next several years.

Almost by default, I became "the Internet guy" in the Syracuse field office, which really wasn't the cool, fun, sexy job to have. While other agents were working bank robberies, drug cases, and chasing down fugitives, I was tracking down eighteen-year-old kids trying to hack into mainframes. To be honest, I'm not sure anyone else in my field office understood what I was doing. Back then, there were very few people who actually owned home computers, and cybercrime was in its infancy. There were only a handful of FBI agents around the country who were involved in these types of cases. They were mostly working investigations that involved young thrill seekers who were trying to gain access to the Pentagon's computer network so they could brag about it to their buddies in online chat rooms.

But cybercrime took a sinister turn in the late 1990s, when American consumers started using credit cards online to pay for goods and services—the beginning of *e-commerce*. When the notorious criminal Willie Sutton was asked why he robbed banks in New York during the 1930s, he simply replied, "Because that's where the money is." Near the end of the twentieth century, a lot of money moved to the Internet, so that's where the bad guys went to commit their crimes. It was up to me to figure out how to stop them. Initially, the phone in our Syracuse field office wasn't ringing off the hook to report cybercrime, so I took a more proactive approach. I identified the largest potential targets in town that bad guys might want to harm. Then I began meeting with different companies and building relationships with the right people in the most vulnerable industries.

In 1998, the FBI made its first attempt to establish a national cyber strategy, which included dedicating one agent in each of the Bureau's fifty-six field offices to computer crime investigations. I was that agent in Syracuse, and I had to devote at least half my working day to investigating computer crimes. There was little guidance from FBI headquarters in Washington, D.C., and working these types of investigations was mostly done by trial and error. On the bright side, though, I was given a laptop, PowerPoint projector, and cellular telephone, which were cutting-edge tools for an FBI agent back then.

The more sophisticated and affordable computers and technology became over the years, the more dangerous things got for American consumers. My workload increased steadily year over year—until 2013, when cybercrime went off the rails. Target, one of America's top retailers, had a mammoth security breach. Hackers obtained the names, credit card numbers, and other sensitive information for about forty million shoppers. My phone didn't stop ringing from that point until I retired from the FBI in January 2018.

If you asked me to define my job today, I would say I teach people and organizations how not to be the victim of a cybercrime incident. I've been able to collaborate with some of the best and brightest people in the private sector to share intelligence, work together on solutions, and keep people safe. I dealt with a lot of large security breaches during my FBI career, and few things were more painful for me than to have to deal with small companies, retirees, and nonprofit organizations that became victims. I now know that providing education to people like them not only serves the community but also keeps us *all* safe.

It was a sad day for me when I retired as a special agent with the FBI. I'd spent more than twenty years working cybercrime cases, and, for seven of those years, I managed one of the best cybercrime units in the U.S. I loved that job. The people I worked with were like family. As an agent, I could have remained employed until I was fifty-seven years old, but I decided to retire when I became eligible at age fifty. Why did I leave something I loved so much? Because, in my heart of hearts, I knew I could do more for the American public from outside the FBI.

Years earlier, I read a book called *Why People Fail,* and the first chapter was about the importance of clarity. Here is what became clear to me at the FBI: I needed to do everything I could to become one of the world's leading experts on cybercrime and risk management. I took a number of classes on information security from the world's leading information security company, and I eventually earned seven information security certifications. It wasn't easy. I read every article I could find about cybercrime, and I talked to as many people in the industry as I could. If you want to become an expert in a certain field, you must invest as much time as possible mastering the subject.

Eventually, I started incorporating what I'd learned into presentations, and I shared what I knew with anyone who would listen. Throughout my FBI career, I delivered thousands of presentations to private-sector companies about how to avoid becoming a victim of cybercrime. As I neared retirement eligibility, I started asking myself, *What do I enjoy doing the most that doesn't feel like work?* The answer was public speaking, educating the public, and meeting new people. These were areas that came naturally to me. It was effortless and fun. That's when I got serious about leaving the Bureau and entering the private sector.

I decided I wanted to change the world by educating small busi-nesses, nonprofits, schools, and public citizens—especially young people and Baby Boomers—about how to avoid becoming victims of computer crimes. With so much money being spent on cybercrime education and prevention, there are very few resources available for the most vulnerable segments of society. I committed myself to taking what I learned during my twenty-nine years in the FBI and sharing it with the public.

In the early days of my FBI career, I measured success by putting bad guys in jail. Today, my success stories happen when somebody calls me after one of my presentations and informs me that they've implemented two-factor authentication on their platforms. If someone had told me when I became an FBI agent that I'd get more job satisfaction from speaking about cybersecurity than arresting bad guys, I would've said, "You're crazy, that's not what I want to do."

Now, it's the *most important* thing I do.

In the pages that follow, I'm going to share a number of steps that, if followed, will reduce your chances of becoming a victim. These action items are not difficult for non-technical folks to understand, and you don't have to spend much money to implement them. Of course, there are only two ways to *guarantee* you won't have to deal with computer crime: move to the Arctic or throw away your computer. You're probably not willing to do either one of those things, and neither am I. However, if you follow these steps, you *will* become a much safer, more protected member of the digital world.

Over the next several chapters, I'm going to share with you several stories that will support each of these steps. And I'm going to be honest with you—I tend to scare people when I talk or write about cybercrime. In the world of information security, there is a term thrown around called *FUD*, which stands for *fear, uncertainty, and doubt.* This term is thrown around by big organizations when someone who tries to explain the scope of the cybercrime problem isn't taken seriously. I've heard people say my lectures are full of FUD. Well, I'm here to introduce a new term called *FFRE*, which stands for *fear from real experience.* Every one of the stories included in this book comes from real-life experience. The victims are real, and the incidents happened. I don't mind taking you out of your comfort zone if it will prevent you from becoming a victim.

CHAPTER 1

Cybercrime

CYBERCRIME HAS BECOME A FACT OF LIFE IN THE DIGITAL world. The threat is incredibly serious—and growing. Cyber-intrusions are becoming more prevalent, more expensive, and far more sophisticated. Our nation's adversaries target our country's critical infrastructure, including utilities, defense systems, and air- and traffic-control mechanisms. U.S. companies are targeted for trade secrets and other sensitive corporate data and universities, for their cutting-edge research and development. Identity thieves are attacking our average citizens, and online predators are stalking our children.

Every day, there is another media report of a large-scale data breach. The American public is becoming numb after hearing the same depressing news over and over. According to analysis conducted by Cybersecurity Ventures, the cost of cybercrime might reach $6 trillion by 2021, doubling in the six years since 2015. A recent study by Dr. Michael McGuire, senior lecturer at the University of Surrey in England, found that cybercrime revenue around the world has grown to $1.5 trillion in illicit profits per year, which is roughly equal to the GDP of Russia! In the U.S., the FBI's Internet Crime Complaint Center received more than three hundred thousand complaints in 2017 with reported losses of more than $1.4 billion.

We have become vulnerable to cybercriminals in nearly every aspect of our lives. If you've ever shopped for home-repair products at The Home Depot (where fifty-six million credit card numbers were compromised from April 2014 to September 2014), purchased clothing or home goods at Target (where hackers infected payment-card readers and made off with approximately forty-one million credit- and debit-card numbers used by after-Thanksgiving shoppers in 2013), or attempted to broaden your professional network by registering at LinkedIn (which had more than six million encrypted passwords stolen by a Russian hacker known as *Peace*, who posted them to a Russian crime forum in May 2016), you might have unknowingly been a victim of cybercrime.

While these massive data breaches involved some of the world's largest companies and made headlines around the world, there was very little media coverage of what I dealt with on a daily basis while fighting cybercrime at the FBI. Every day, I worked with victims at small- and medium-sized businesses, nonprofit organizations, academic institutions, and, even worse, with retirees who lost their life savings. I witnessed too many horror stories during my career—including several businesses that were forced to close their doors after being victims of cybercrimes. Here are a few of the crimes I investigated during my FBI career:

DIANE, A MOTHER OF TWO FROM FRANKLIN, TENNESSEE, came home from a long day at the office. She made dinner for her family, took a shower, and then logged on to her laptop. She still preferred to check her email on her computer and rarely accessed it on her iPhone; she preferred the much larger screen. Her fourteen-year-old daughter liked to tease her about using the aging computer, saying it made her old in the rapidly changing digital world.

As Diane went through her Gmail account, she quickly deleted spam and advertisements and then noticed an email from her sister, Abigail. Diane's sister regularly sent her articles about health and fitness, and this email seemed to be no different. The email included a hyperlink to an article about the benefits of drinking coconut water and its ability to reduce wrinkles. Diane always read the articles her sister sent, so she clicked the link about coconut water and waited for the article to appear. Nothing happened. She clicked again. No response. She figured her Internet service must be running slow again, which was the cause of most of her computer problems. She grew tired of waiting, read the rest of her emails, browsed a few of her favorite online retailers, and then it was time to watch the latest episode of *The Walking Dead*.

Diane fought to keep her eyes open as Rick Grimes and his ragtag group tried to survive a zombie apocalypse on TV. Meanwhile, a zombie computer halfway around the world in Eastern Europe was talking to her computer. When Diane clicked the hyperlink to the article about coconut water, she was redirected to a computer controlled by a cybercriminal. Once connected, the computer loaded a malicious program called a keylogger onto Diane's machine. A keylogger, sometimes called a keystroke logger or system monitor, has one job: to monitor and record each keystroke typed on a specific computer's keyboard. When Diane entered a username and password for a website, such as Gmail, her work email account, or online banking account, the malicious keylogger program stole her credentials and sent them to the cybercriminal, who now had access to Diane's websites. Once the bad guy obtained access to Diane's bank account, he was ready to wipe out her savings.

JONATHAN WAS A RETIRED HIGH SCHOOL TEACHER WITH A love for writing and poetry. His pension covered his living expenses, and he supplemented his retirement income with his salary from a side business as a wedding photographer. Whenever Jonathan wasn't taking photographs, he spent his time writing. He finally hatched an idea for a novel, which he believed was the idea of a lifetime. It took him eighteen months to write seventy-five thousand words, but he finally finished. He considered the crime novel to be his life's work and was about to become a published author through Amazon self-publishing.

One weekend, Jonathan was working as a photographer at a ritzy wedding. It was a black-tie affair, and he couldn't believe how much money he was going to make in one night. It was hard work, but he'd earn as much in one night as he made in one *week* as a teacher. Once Jonathan returned home from the wedding, he downloaded the photos to his computer and started editing them with his photo-editing software. When he was finished, he saved the photos to his hard drive. Before going to bed, Jonathan checked his Facebook account and clicked on a link from an individual who wanted to become his online friend. It was from an attractive young woman who commented on Jonathan's exceptional photography skills.

Halfway around the world, there was a cybercriminal sitting in front of a laptop in Eastern Europe. Let's call him Ivan. Ivan smiled as soon as Jonathan clicked on the link. He knew an unsuspecting American was about to have his world turned upside down. One of Ivan's zombie computers had sent thousands of spear-phishing emails disguised as spam messages on Facebook. He targeted male Facebook users and offered to friend the unsuspecting victims. Ivan claimed to be an attractive woman who was impressed with an interest that was listed on the men's Facebook pages. It was like taking candy from a baby. When Jonathan clicked on the link, Ivan's computer encrypted all the information on his hard drive. Jonathan couldn't regain access to his photographs or manuscript unless he paid Ivan a ransom of $300. Making matters worse, Ivan's malicious program also targeted Jonathan's Apple iCloud account and changed all his passwords. Even if Jonathan had previously backed up his information to iCloud (he didn't), he wouldn't be able to retrieve it now without paying the ransom.

IT WAS A TYPICAL MONDAY MORNING FOR HEATHER, A newly hired payroll clerk at a large company, when she received an email from her CEO. He asked if she was enjoying her new job, commended her on her work so far, and told her that the payroll manager believed she was on the fast track for a promotion. Heather was overjoyed that the CEO knew her and believed she was doing a great job. The email also included some instructions for Heather: Since the payroll manager was out of town at a business conference, he needed her to complete a special project. The CEO was headed to a meeting with the company's board of directors and needed a spreadsheet that included every employee's name, title, birthday, address, Social Security number, and salary. Heather was eager for added responsibility and replied that she'd complete the task within the hour. She added the personal information of more than two thousand employees to an Excel spreadsheet and attached it to an email she sent to the CEO. At least that's what she believed was happening.

In a dirty Internet café in West Africa, a cybercriminal received Heather's email, jumped out of his chair, and started celebrating. One of his spear-phished emails went to a payroll clerk in America requesting the W-2 information for a large company's payroll. The unsuspecting payroll clerk sent him back the sensitive personal information of more than two thousand employees. In a room full of other cybercriminals, the man announced that he was selling the names, birthdays, Social Security numbers, addresses, and salaries for $5 each. The other cybercriminals started handing him money like he was a trader on Wall Street. In only twenty minutes, the villain walked away with more than $5,000. Within months, his criminal customers attempted to file federal tax returns for the victimized employees and access their credit card accounts.

CAROLINE WAS A TWENTY-ONE-YEAR-OLD COLLEGE junior and was not having a great week. Midterms were fast approaching, she'd just had an ugly fight with her boyfriend, and her parents were upset that she'd recently been pulled over for speeding. They knew their insurance premiums were about to skyrocket. As Caroline prepared to leave for her next class, her cell phone rang. The caller ID indicated the call was coming from the local police department. Immediately, Caroline had a sick feeling in her stomach as she answered the phone. The caller identified himself as Detective Miller with the police department. He asked Caroline why she hadn't yet responded to letters from the police that identified her as a driver running through a red light. He said the letters included a photograph taken by a traffic camera. Caroline told the officer that she hadn't received the letter. The officer advised her that three letters had been sent to her campus address and that a warrant had been issued for her arrest. Her driver's license was also going to be suspended for failing to appear in court. Caroline reached her breaking point and broke down in tears.

Miller seemed to take pity on Caroline and told her that she sounded like a nice girl. If she was willing to pay $250 in fines that day, he advised her, the violation would be removed from her driving record and her license wouldn't be suspended. Caroline was relieved and told the officer that she'd come to the station later that day to pay the fines. But Miller told her that, since the violation was with the state police, she needed to go to Walmart and send a Western Union money order immediately. He then provided her with instructions on where to send the money.

Somewhere in the United States, a cybercriminal climbed off his couch, put on his pants, and drove to his local Walmart to receive $250. His life had changed for the better ever since he watched a YouTube video with instructions on how to make money quickly. The only thing he had to do was find people who had posted information about traffic tickets on their Facebook pages; after that, it wasn't too difficult to obtain their telephone numbers. It was an easy way to make a living, and most of his victims were relieved to get off so cheaply. At least they wouldn't lose their driver's license or go to jail—not that this was ever even possible in this scenario.

MICHAEL WAS THE OWNER OF A SUCCESSFUL SERVICES company. He was happily married, had two beautiful children, and was active in his church. One night, Michael received an enticing Facebook message from a woman with an exotic Asian name. Against Michael's better judgment, he exchanged emails with the woman. They engaged in a few online conversations and got to know each other. At some point, she suggested they could talk to each other via Skype. Within five minutes, Michael was looking at a beautiful, young blonde woman, who appeared to be between twenty and twenty-five years old. She told him her name was Melania, and that she was from South Africa.

Somewhere in a remote village in Asia, members of a cybercrime extortion ring were putting their plan into action. The only thing left to do was push a button and record Michael's Skype call. Michael locked the door of his office to give himself a little privacy; he didn't know he was being video-recorded. Before long, Melania took off her clothes and started performing sex acts. She told Michael she wanted him to do the same thing. He did. After the call, he logged off and went back to work.

A few minutes later, Michael received an email from Melania, in which she told him she needed $10,000 to pay her mother's medical bills. She had no choice but to demand the money from Michael to save her dying mother. A link to a private YouTube channel of Michael's video was included in the email. The video's quality was excellent, and there was no room for doubt that it was Michael who was unclothed and doing things he shouldn't have been doing. Melania warned Michael that, if he didn't send her the money, a link to the video would be sent to his Facebook friends, including his wife, children, fellow church members, and business associates.

Michael should have contacted law enforcement after receiving the ransom letter, but he didn't. Although losing $10,000 would be a very expensive lesson, Michael believed it was a bargain to avoid public humiliation. He went to his bank and made a wire transfer to a bank in Russia. The location seemed odd to him since Melania claimed she was from South Africa, but he had been assured the video would be destroyed once the ransom was paid. He felt relieved to have dodged a bullet that might have destroyed his marriage and career and ruined his reputation for life.

Michael still felt relieved when he woke up the next morning. It almost seemed like a bad dream. But, when he checked his email, he found another message from Melania. She apologized and said the $10,000 he'd sent wasn't enough. She needed him to transfer an additional $35,000 to the same bank account. Michael was furious and sent her an angry email, saying she hadn't lived up to her end of the deal. She emailed him back immediately and reminded him what would happen if he didn't pay. Michael didn't think he had a choice, so he sent Melania another $35,000 that afternoon. Over the next several weeks, Michael sent her a total of $150,000.

By the time Michael called the FBI office, he was at the end of his rope. He was humiliated, had wiped out most of his retirement savings, and was actually considering suicide. I'm convinced the bad guys wouldn't have stopped making demands until they'd drained every penny from Michael or, worse, he'd killed himself.

PATRICK WAS TWENTY-FIVE YEARS OLD AND NEWLY married when he and his wife saved $50,000 for a down payment on their first home. After numerous meetings, telephone calls, and emails, Patrick and his wife selected what they thought was their dream home. Shortly before closing on the property, Patrick's broker told him he was only waiting for instructions from the title company about where to wire his down payment. A few hours later, Patrick received an email from a title company with detailed wire transfer instructions, including a bank account and routing number. Patrick went to his bank and withdrew his hard-earned $50,000. He provided the wire instructions to a bank official and left one step closer to becoming a first-time home buyer—or so he thought.

The next day, Patrick received an email from the actual title company with instructions on where to send the money. Obviously confused because he'd wired the money the previous day, Patrick emailed his broker. Patrick and his broker called the title company, and it took a while for everyone to get on the same page. The title company informed Patrick that it hadn't sent the previous day's email. Looking carefully at the title company's instructions, Patrick became concerned that the routing number and bank account number were different than the ones from the previous day. Upon closer inspection, he also noticed the name of the title company was slightly altered in the email address in the earlier emails. Patrick called his bank to stop the wire transfer, but it was too late. An official from Patrick's bank called someone from the bank where the money was sent, but the funds had already been withdrawn.

Obviously panicked about losing so much money, Patrick called the title company. Its attorney informed him, in a nice way, that it wasn't responsible because it hadn't sent the original email. Patrick contacted the local police, who told him the bank that received the money was located in another state and therefore out of its jurisdiction. Patrick called the state police, who told him it didn't have the necessary resources to investigative cybercrime. He was instructed to notify the FBI, which directed him to go to the www.IC3.gov website and fill out a complaint to the FBI's Internet Crime Complaint Center. As far as I know, Patrick is still trying to recover his money.

NOT LONG AGO, A WEALTHY OLDER GENTLEMAN NAMED David was comparing rates for certificates of deposits on the Internet. He found a bank in California that was offering a competitive rate; it wasn't a *great* rate, but it was better than what local banks were offering. David was interested in investing a sizable amount of money, so even a quarter of a percentage point could mean a few thousand dollars in interest earned. David contacted the bank and spoke to a representative, who was pleasant and knowledgeable on the phone. During their conversation, the bank rep persuaded David to send $750,000 to the bank via wire transfer. David followed the man's instructions and received a confirmation email.

David didn't hear from anyone from the California bank for a few days, so he called the number he'd originally dialed. No one answered. When he tried to go to the bank's website on the Internet, it was no longer there. He started to become concerned and contacted someone at his bank, which discovered his money hadn't been sent to a bank in California but instead to one in Georgia—the *country* in Eastern Europe, not the state in the American Southeast The FBI's legal attaché in Georgia was contacted, and our law enforcement partners there were notified. Unfortunately, David never got his money back, and the bad guys didn't go to jail.

I wish these stories were fiction, but every one of them happened during my tenure with the FBI. The names were changed to protect the victims' identities, but the facts are accurate. They are scary scenarios and most individuals feel helpless when cybercriminals victimize them. In a lot of instances, I heard the same response from victims: "I'm a small businessman, and I don't have the money to spend on online security. I'm not technology proficient."

I spent twenty-nine years in the FBI, six as a support employee and twenty-three as a special agent. My last fourteen years were spent investigating cybercrime. If you were hoping to read a book about how FBI agents took down a large group of cybercriminals, I'm sorry to disappoint you. There are a lot of great FBI agents who tell entertaining stories about arresting bad guys over the course of their careers; unfortunately, I don't have a lot of those stories to tell. The criminals I chased around the world don't get caught very often. That's why it's so important to learn how to cut them off *before* the crime ever happens.

CHAPTER 2

THE FOUR TRUTHS

IN 2002, THE FBI FORMED A CYBER DIVISION AT ITS HEAD-quarters in Washington, D.C., and a national strategy was developed to combat the emerging threat of computer crimes. Part of my job as a special agent in Syracuse, New York, was to handle all cyber matters, and one of my responsibilities was to inform the public of the FBI's mission in this investigative area. I still remember the highlights from my presentations to the public in 2001. I had a slide titled "Why the Increase in Cybercrime?" that warned:

1. There was little risk for criminals of actually being caught, because the bad guys were behind keyboards and didn't have to stick a gun in your face to steal your money.
2. Attribution was difficult to prove because once you were able to identify the computer behind the crimes, you still had to prove the person behind the computer was the one actually committing the crime.
3. There was a lack of experienced law enforcement investigators, prosecutors, and judges dealing with computer crimes. It was diffi-cult to establish judicial venue if the bad guy was located in New York and the victim or victims were located throughout the U.S. or other parts of the world.
4. There were no boundaries in cyberspace and bad guys from around the world could access our critical information. Many foreign governments were not concerned if criminals from their countries were victimizing U.S. citizens. Many of those countries refused to cooperate with the U.S. government in investigations.
5. More and more people were purchasing home computers and had access to email, e-commerce, and online banking. With more people accessing the World Wide Web, suddenly almost everyone had an email account.

What has changed since then? Everyone has a home computer and today's cell phones and tablets are much more powerful than the home computers of 2002. We can do so many things on our cell phones now—watch movies, music videos, and live sporting events;

check email; log in to our corporate networks; pay our mortgages and other bills; and purchase goods from around the world. The bad guys of the early Internet have changed from teenage hackers living in their parents' basements to financially motivated, foreign-based adversaries who have ties to organized crime. Through social media accounts like Facebook, Instagram, Twitter, and others, we have provided those who want to do us harm with too much information about our personal lives, our families, and our employers. The only thing the bad guys have to do now is Google our names and they'll find a plethora of information they can use against us.

In 2002, it took a lot of skill to become a cybercriminal. Today, the necessary tools are available to almost anyone online. *Crimeware* is a term used by law enforcement to describe the tools needed by crooks to commit cybercrime—and these tools are readily available at a low cost. There is a part of the Internet called the *dark web* that exists on darknets and overlay networks and requires special software and routers to access. The dark web is usually encrypted content and isn't indexed on conventional search engines. This is where criminals sell drugs, hack software, counterfeit money, and more. It's also the place where stolen classified information is brokered and traded by hackers, and it's where human traffickers conduct their abhorrent work.

Unfortunately, the software and routers needed to access the dark web can be easily purchased. You can buy other types of destructive cyber-tools and methods for hiding your tracks and make it almost impossible for anyone to hunt you down. The illegal theft and release of hacking tools used by the National Security Agency (NSA) made matters much worse in August 2016. A hacking group called the Shadow Brokers stole the tools the NSA used to keep our country safe from terrorists and foreign intelligence services and posted them online. Now, the very tools originally designed to protect us are being used in a number of cyberattacks around the world.

During the past fifteen years, I was involved in thousands of cybercrime cases, and I noticed the same four qualities in each instance. I now call these the Four Truths:

1. Truth One: Nobody expects to become a victim.

I heard it over and over again during my career in law enforcement: *I'm a small CPA firm. I'm a nonprofit. I'm a small healthcare company. I don't have anything a cybercriminal would want to steal.* I once had the CEO of a nonprofit organization tell me that no one would ever target a nonprofit. What would they want to steal? The bad news is that I worked with dozens of nonprofits that were victimized. Nonprofits collect sensitive data, including donor information, health information, Social Security numbers, confidential emails, employee and volunteer records, and billing information.

One of the worst incidents involving a nonprofit that I've heard about involved the Little Red Door, an organization that helps women battling cancer in Muncie, Indiana. A group of hackers infected the nonprofit's computers with malware (software intentionally designed to cause damage to a computer, server, or computer network) in January 2017, and its staff members couldn't access patient files and other information. The hackers held the information hostage and wanted fifty bitcoin—an emerging online currency worth about $43,000 at the time—to release the files. At one point, the hackers even sent an email to the nonprofit that read, "Cancer sucks, but we suck more!" The bad guys are heartless. The Little Red Door couldn't pay the ransom, so its staff members had to reload patients' information into computers.

There are disturbing signs that hackers are increasingly targeting nonprofits and small businesses because they are less likely to have sophisticated security measures. Data breaches can be especially damaging to nonprofits because they lead to lost time, litigation, fines, and penalties—as well as a loss of public trust, which can have a negative effect on donor contributions. The same goes for churches. One leader of a religious organization actually told me that God was its firewall and no one would ever target a church. Again, that's not true. Churches and nonprofits have bank accounts that are accessible via the Internet, and I have seen them victimized on numerous occasions.

Nonprofits and religious organizations aren't the only groups that are naïve when it comes to the growing dangers of cybercrime. I've had conversations with executives of publicly traded companies on the NASDAQ exchange who have told me they weren't worried about cybersecurity; they said the bad guys were only targeting companies on the New York Stock Exchange (NYSE)! Recently, an executive of a publicly traded company on the NYSE told me he wasn't concerned because his organization's annual revenue was less than $5 billion, and the cyberthieves were only targeting companies with revenues of more than $30 billion! Of course, that isn't true, and those types of attitudes are a big part of the cybercrime problem.

All of us, whether we work for a publicly traded corporation with billions of dollars in annual revenue or a small nonprofit that is struggling to keep its doors open, have information cybercriminals want to get their hands on. When a thief obtains the username and password for our bank accounts, there's a good chance he's going to drain our funds. If he gets access to our computer files and finds something sensitive, such as our tax returns, he is going to use that information to open credit card or loan accounts in our name and make us victims of identify theft. If he gets access to our email and social media accounts, he is going to use what he learns about us as a weapon to gain access to even more victims.

During one of my cybersecurity presentations, a woman interrupted me and said she had nothing at all to worry about. She didn't bank online and only used her bank's website to check her account balances. When I asked her if she needed a username and password to access her balance, she confirmed that she did. I asked her to log in to her account and pull up the automated bill-pay tool, where she could enter an account and routing number to make payments. She told me she didn't use the bill-pay feature and said in a particularly condescending tone, "I only check my bank balance." But then I asked her what would happen if the bad guys gained access to her bank account, username, and password, and then entered the stolen information to make a payment to themselves. At this point, she finally understood how vulnerable she really was—along with the rest of the American public.

I always like to ask people at my cybersecurity safety presentations to identify the most important data they've stored on their computers.

If you're an author, it's probably an unfinished manuscript. If you're a student, it might be a thesis paper or homework. If you're a small business, it's human resources materials or banking records. If a cybercriminal were to break into your computer, what's the *one thing* you wouldn't want him to steal? I get a variety of answers from people in the audience, and then I like to joke, "Did someone say naked photographs?" Whatever information is important to you is important to a thief. That makes every one of us a target.

2. Truth Two: You're probably not getting your money back.

This might be the most difficult concept for people to understand: When cybercriminals gain access to your bank account and steal all your money, law enforcement's chances of recouping your money is really slim to none. I hate to say that, but it's true. Don't get me wrong; I have a few success stories of recovering money that left the U.S. in compromised business email scams. If there were a Hall of Fame for FBI agents who recovered money that ended up overseas, my name would probably be on a plaque hanging on a wall. But the cold truth is that I'd probably be hitting below .100, and that's not going to get me anywhere close to the Baseball Hall of Fame in Cooperstown, New York.

I recently spoke at a conference and told the crowd about how difficult it is for law enforcement to recover money from foreign cybercriminals. A retired FBI executive was speaking at the same conference, and he criticized me for telling the audience that law enforcement, particularly the FBI, probably can't get their property back. I smiled at him and said, "The truth hurts, doesn't it?" He looked stunned.

Unfortunately, it's absolutely the truth in a lot of cases. A 2017 study by the cybersecurity company Kaspersky Lab found that 52 percent of people surveyed reported recovering either none or only some of their money that was stolen in computer crimes. On average, the study found, Internet users lost $476 per attack and one in ten people reported losing more than $5,000. Even more surprising, 81 percent of the respondents reported conducting financial transactions online and 44 percent admitted storing financial data on their connected devices. However, only 60 percent of Internet users reported protecting all of their devices with cybersecurity software. You might as well email your usernames and passwords to the cybercriminals!

3. Truth Three: The bad guys probably aren't getting arrested.
One of the most frustrating parts of cybercrime is that it's so prevalent, yet there are so few arrests. The big problem is that computer criminals aren't always based in the U.S. In many cases, the cybercriminal who infects your computer to steal your personal information is based somewhere in Eastern Europe, West Africa, Asia, South America, or the Middle East.

According to the cybersecurity company Symantec, the countries that were the largest sources of malware, spam, and phishing in 2017 were the U.S. (23.96 percent), China (9.63 percent), Brazil (5.84 percent), India (5.11 percent), Germany (3.35 percent), Russia (3.07 percent), United Kingdom (2.61 percent), France (2.35 percent), Japan (2.25 percent), and Vietnam (2.16 percent). While the FBI and other law-enforcement agencies will obviously have a better chance of identifying and arresting homegrown hackers, it's much more difficult for them to locate and apprehend computer-based criminals operating overseas. Many cybercriminals are based in countries like China and Russia for a specific reason—the governments there aren't friendly to the U.S. and aren't likely to cooperate in an investigation or extradite their citizens to face punishment for crimes. When I first started working with the FBI, fighting crime was a localized problem; now, it's an international problem.

In the past couple of years, the FBI has arrested and prosecuted some high-level criminals based overseas, and the FBI agents assigned to cybercrime are working overtime to make arrests. There have been a few notable success stories in recent years. In December 2016, a computer hacker named Mark Vartanya, also known as *Kolypto*, was extradited from Norway to the U.S. for his role as a Citadel malware toolkit co-developer. He helped steal financial account credentials and personal information from eleven million infected computers around the world, resulting in more than $500 million in losses. He pleaded guilty and was sentenced to five years in prison. In February 2018, the

U.S. Justice Department announced charges against more than thirty individuals who were key members of *Infraud*, a long-running online cybercrime forum. The fraud forum attracted more than eleven thousand members from around the world who sold, traded, and purchased stolen identities, credit card accounts, and malicious software, costing consumers worldwide more than $500 million in losses.

I hate to say this, but we're not going to arrest our way out of the cybercrime problem. There are many safe havens for computer criminals around the world, and the host governments in many of these places simply aren't concerned that their citizens are victimizing people in the U.S. If you go to the FBI website and look at the most wanted list of cybercriminals (www.fbi.gov/wanted/cyber), you will see twenty-five names you probably can't pronounce. If any of them jumped on a plane and headed for vacation in Daytona Beach, Florida, I promise you that FBI agents would apprehend them at the airport. But if you believe any of the cybercriminals are going to travel to the U.S., then I have a bridge to sell you in Brooklyn.

This is the moment when it's okay for you to become depressed. You've just discovered that there's very little chance you're getting your money back when the bad guys steal your stuff and you notify law enforcement. And then I told you law enforcement's chance of arresting and punishing the bad guys is probably even slimmer than you getting your money back. I broke that news at an event where liquor was being served, and a guy yelled from the crowd, "No wonder the president fired FBI director [James] Comey! What do you guys really do?" Obviously, my former position required having thick skin. This leads me to my fourth and final point, which is what drove me to write this book in an attempt to educate the American public.

4. Truth Four: A majority of cybercrime can be prevented.

I made this point to a friend of mine who is a senior executive at FBI headquarters in Washington, D.C. He sharply disagreed with my assessment, as do many others on a regular basis. When I make that statement, I get depressed because I know 90 percent of the cases I investigated might have been prevented through user education and awareness, sound business processes, and the use of a simple control called two-factor authentication. My FBI colleague explained that foreign intelligence services from China and Russia are using extremely sophisticated techniques and, when these threat actors target an organization or individual, the bad guys will win every single time. In some cases, that's a true statement. I've seen these threat actors target some of the largest organizations in the world and gain access. But there are also plenty of unsophisticated threats from all around the world that are jumping on the bandwagon. They are victimizing senior citizens, homeowners, small businesses, and nonprofits and causing grave damage. Large companies have money to throw at the problem, but it's not working.

In 2017, Cybersecurity Ventures predicted that cybercrime would cost the world $6 trillion annually by 2021, up from $3 trillion only two years before. That represents the greatest transfer of economic wealth in history, according to the Herjavec Group. Amazingly, cybercrime will be more profitable than the global trade of all illegal drugs combined. Incidents of cybercrime are continuing to occur at an alarming rate and more and more data is being stolen. We're spending an increasing amount money to stop it too. Garner Inc. says worldwide information security costs climbed to $93 billion in 2018 and will climb to more than $1 trillion by 2021—and we're barely making a dent in preventing it. The fact that nearly every household appliance or piece of electronics will be connected to the Internet in the very near future leads me to believe that things are only going to get worse.

During the final ten years of my FBI career, I dissected more than one thousand cybercrime incidents and data breaches. There were commonalities in each of the incidents, and I came up with a list of precautions that, if followed, will dramatically reduce your chances of becoming a victim. I'm going to refer to my points as methods of improving your cyber-hygiene. What I'm going to share with you won't cost a lot of money either. In fact, the majority of my techniques will seem like common sense.

Unfortunately, there's no magic pill or silver bullet that will keep you safe. However, a combination of available techniques will greatly reduce your risk. If a cybersecurity salesman comes to your organization and says he has a product that will keep you safe and protect you from every single threat out there, I have news for you: he's lying. There's no single product on the market that will eliminate all the risk; cyber-criminals simply work too fast and the threats are constantly changing. There is a term for this in our industry: *Defense in Depth.* This means not relying on *one* product for safety. Using only one strategy or no strategy is bad cyber-hygiene, and I can promise you one thing: if you don't have good cyber-hygiene, the odds are stacked against you. You're going to be hacked, and cybercriminals are probably going to get their greasy hands on your money.

Before I go into the techniques, I have to admit that I didn't create or develop any of these techniques. I've just been lucky—or should I say *unlucky*—to have witnessed and investigated thousands of cyber-crime incidents and identify their root causes. Hopefully, I can use what I learned to make you safer on the Internet.

CHAPTER 3

Phishing

IT SEEMS LIKE ONLY YESTERDAY WHEN I STUCK AN AMERICA
Online CD into my laptop, plugged a cable into a telephone jack on the
wall, and was connected to the information superhighway—now known
as the Internet—for the first time.

The World Wide Web was invented in 1989 (no, not by Al Gore) and
the first website went live in 1991. Within a few years, I was emailing my
friends on a regular basis and exchanging photos with them. By 1998,
when Tom Hanks and Meg Ryan starred in the Hollywood hit *You've Got
Mail*, the world was hooked on the Internet and everybody was using
email. It was so easy that even our parents, grandparents, and children
had the ability to send email. Today, there are more than 3.8 billion email
users (more than half the planet's entire population), according to a
2018 study by the Radicati Group. That number is predicted to climb to
4.2 billion by 2022. Since the average person has 1.7 email accounts,
some for personal use and others for business, there are around 4.4
billion accounts worldwide.

But around the time AOL, Amazon, and eBay were becoming
household names, something sinister was brewing beneath the surface
of the Internet. In 2005, I lived in Washington, D.C., and worked in
the Cyber Division at FBI headquarters. I remember being home one
evening in 2005 and receiving an email from a large bank. The email
appeared official; it said there was a problem and that my bank account
had been frozen. In order to regain access to the account, the email
instructed me to click a link and enter my username, password, birth-
date, and Social Security number on the webpage that appeared. There
was only one problem: I didn't have an account at this specific bank!
Obviously confused, I immediately called the bank's customer service
department and explained the situation. The person on the phone told
me he couldn't help unless I had a valid account. Even after I explained
to him that I was an FBI special agent who investigated cybercrime, the
customer service representative told me, "Sorry, I can't help unless you
have a valid account."

I wonder how many unsuspecting people received that email and
provided their account credentials to Eastern European cybercriminals,
who undoubtedly drained their accounts. Somewhere in the former

Russian Federation, a crook was probably sitting behind a keyboard. He had a name that sounded like Boris Badenov, the villain on the old TV cartoon *The Adventures of Rocky and Bullwinkle and Friends*. Boris was smiling because he'd figured out one of the world's easiest scams. If Boris called you on the phone today and asked you for your username and password with his deep Russian accent, you would surely hang up on him. So Boris would probably go to Plan B. He'd send you an email asking for the information, but he's not dumb enough to send it from an email address like borisbadenov@cybercriminal.com. This isn't some teenage hacker living in his mother's basement; he's a sophisticated cybercriminal, someone who might be connected to a foreign government or an organized crime outfit. Boris might even have a friend who's a graphic designer, and he's probably talented enough to design a website that looks exactly like the one your bank uses.

Boris is now engaged in the act of *phishing*, which is not to be confused with the sport of fishing. Put simply, phishing is the fraudulent practice of sending emails purporting to be from reputable companies in order to steal personal information such as passwords, usernames, and credit card numbers. According to IBM's X-Force researchers, more than half of all emails sent everyday are spam. The Radicati Group estimates that 269 billion emails were sent and received every day in 2017 and that number will climb to 319.6 billion by the end of 2021. When there are that many phish in the sea, it's easy to see why criminals are so successful.

During my cybercrime presentations, I ask the audience this question: If you received an email from your bank under the previous circumstances, is there anyone in the audience who would provide their banking credentials? Of course, almost everyone in the room pipes up with a great big *no!* Then I ask them about their iTunes, Amazon, Facebook, eBay, Google, and Instagram accounts. If you received an email asking for your credentials from one of those providers, would you provide them? Today, almost everyone knows not to provide credentials when asked in an email from any provider. But I can't tell you how many times I've spoken at a high school or college, or even a civic group, and been surprised at the exasperated looks on people's faces when I explain this point. It's like they're hearing it for the first time! If you provide your credentials to *any* of these accounts, the bad guy will gain access to the account and cause havoc. When I'm doing my presentation, I make people repeat this sentence: *I will never provide my credentials to any provider when requested in an email.* This is a concept I've explained to my kids, and I'm sure I could even explain it to my elderly mother—but she doesn't need an explanation. I never purchased a computer for my mom and, when I finally bought her a cell phone ten years ago, I never upgraded her to a phone with an Internet connection. Some might say I'm being cruel and have deprived her of one of life's great luxuries, but I've seen too many of my friends' parents become cyber-victims.

Over the past ten years, there have been a number of public-service campaigns warning people about the dangers of phishing. Sadly, cyber-criminals don't quit easily; they simply change their techniques to trick unsuspecting individuals into giving up their usernames and passwords. As computer users become more educated and security software and firewalls become more effective in protecting them from intrusions, cybercriminals simply create different malware. Malware does its dirty work after it's implanted or introduced to a computer or network. It can implant computer viruses, worms, Trojan horses, ransomware, spyware, adware, scareware, and who knows what else. Malware has been around for as long as computers have been in use. The first Trojan was released in 1978, the first virus for Apple systems in 1983, and the first virus for IBM PC computers in 1986.

Some malware installs a keystroke logger, which I mentioned in Chapter 1. Once the keystrokes are captured, the program sends the information back to an online server, which a cybercriminal can access to steal your personal information. The Soviet Union first developed and deployed a hardware keylogger back in the mid-1970s, when it installed them on IBM Selectric typewriters. The keystroke loggers were covertly installed at U.S. embassies and consulate buildings in Moscow and St. Petersburg to steal classified information. Because manual typewriters are immune to keyloggers and other viruses, the Russian special services are still using them today!

One keylogging case I encountered during my FBI career involved a man named Charlie who was an attorney at a midsized firm. He received an email to his personal email account from what appeared to be his bank. The subject line said, "Suspicious Activity Detected On Your Account." Charlie opened the email, which read:

Dear Charlie, we would like to inform you that our bank's new security system has detected a possibly suspicious transaction about to be processed through your checking account. Today at 9:05 A.M., a login was detected into your account from an IP address in Brooklyn, New York. The user requested an automated withdraw from your bank account in the amount of $1,875.54 payable to an online casino in the Bahamas.

Charlie's blood pressure spiked dramatically after he read the first few sentences of the email. He could feel a pit of anxiety in his stomach. The cybercriminal had baited the hook in his phishing attempt and now had Charlie dangling on the end of the line. It was time to reel him in:

If this is a legitimate transaction, there is no need to do anything at all. The funds will be withdrawn from your account within the next hour. If you did not authorize this transaction, please contact the bank within the next hour. Your failure to contact the bank will result in monies being withdrawn from your account. To prevent this transaction from taking place, all you need to do is click on the link in this email or call the toll-free number below.

This what I describe as the Jedi mind trick.

When I use this example during one of my presentations, I always ask the audience, "What would the majority of the population do in this situation?" When I ask that question, the audience usually remains silent. But when I ask the question indirectly, they always seem to have the same answer: "Click on the link." There are typically a few individuals who give me a look that says, "I would never click the link. Instead, I would call the toll-free number in the email." That's just as bad. When you call the number, you'll probably be talking to someone in the Ukraine, who might speak English without an accent, and he's going to instruct you to click the link. Repeat after me: *I will never call the telephone number in the email and will always maintain a list of telephone numbers for my banks and providers.*

Now, if Charlie clicks on the link in the email, he is playing directly into Boris's hands. He will be redirected to a computer outside the U.S. that is being controlled by Boris and other criminals. Two things typically happen at this point: If a keystroke logger has been installed, Boris can steal Charlie's username and password for his bank account. Or, Charlie will believe he has landed on his bank's website, and he'll be greeted with a webpage that has instructions for stopping the fraudulent transaction. All he has to do is enter his username and password. The only thing Charlie is worried about is protecting his money, so he'll gladly log in to the bank's website to prevent it from happening. Once he enters his username and password, the keylogging software captures them, and now Boris has the information he needs to access Charlie's account.

But there might be one more step in this scenario. Once Boris logs into the bank's actual website with Charlie's username and password, the bank's computer will probably recognize that someone is logging in from an unknown computer and IP address. So the bank's website presents an additional hurdle—a security question. There are many forms of security questions, from your mother's maiden name, first pet, high school mascot, to the maid of honor or best man at your wedding. Consider security questions on your bank's website and ask yourself, *Could Boris or another criminal find the answers to my challenge questions by examining my social media accounts or searching my name in Google?* Sadly, the answer is a resounding *yes* for most people.

You might remember when Alaska governor and Republican vice-presidential candidate Sarah Palin had her Yahoo! email account compromised during the height of the 2008 U.S. presidential election. The hacker known as *Rubico* was actually David Kernell, a twenty-year-old college student from the University of Tennessee and son of a Tennessee state representative. According to federal authorities, Kernell unlawfully accessed Palin's email account because he was searching for something to derail her campaign. Since Knoxville, Tennessee, wasn't included in my jurisdiction, I wasn't involved in the case. For the record, though, Palin's account wasn't *hacked*. Hacking involves using technology to unlawfully access someone else's account. Palin's account was accessed by someone else because she used weak security questions. In fact, Kernell told federal authorities that he answered Palin's security questions in about "fifteen seconds." Her security questions included her birthday, high school, and high school mascot. Kernell found her birthday on her Wikipedia page, and it was easy to determine her high school and high school mascot because she grew up in the small town of Wasilla, Alaska. It was that easy. Kernell was found guilty of one felony count of anticipatory obstruction of justice (he tried to destroy computer evidence) and one misdemeanor count of unauthorized access of a computer in 2010. He was sentenced to one year plus one day in a minimum-security prison.

Hopefully, Palin learned to use more difficult security questions. In many instances, security questions are the last line of defense in online security. They are the only things preventing Boris Badenov and other cybercriminals from gaining access to your accounts. I'm the parent of two teenagers, and I've taught them the importance of telling the truth. Integrity, honesty, and kindness are three of the most important attributes we can teach our children. But I don't want my kids telling the truth when it comes to online security questions. I don't want them sharing their birthdates, hometowns, best friend's names, or high school mascots on the Internet. A cybercriminal can easily find the answers through social media or online search engines, given how much information we share about our families and ourselves nowadays.

The trick to answering online security questions is coming up with answers that are easy to remember, yet difficult for the bad guys to guess. Use answers that involve things like your favorite foods, cars, vacation spots, or brand names of appliances. For instance, your best friend's name could be "pizza," your high school could be "barbeque ribs," and your mother's maiden name might be "fried chicken." Use your imagination. Just don't use any answers that might be figured out by searching your Facebook page or other information that is easily accessible online.

After you've come up with creative and unique answers to security questions, write them down and keep them in a secure place. Never store them on your computers, tablets, or cell phones. And don't do what I did! One day, I called my bank to handle a transaction and a customer service representative asked for my mother's maiden name. I wasn't thinking and provided her actual maiden name. The customer service representative told me my answer was incorrect and the tone of her voice changed dramatically. It's a red flag when someone can't remember his mother's maiden name. I then remembered that I'd used the names of appliances in my security answers, so I told her my mother's maiden name was Maytag. Wrong again. I rattled off Kenmore, Viking, and GE, before she quickly transferred me to the bank's security department. Fortunately, the security representative had a sense of humor. He laughed when I told him that I'd used appliance brands for my answers and then he gave me some really good advice: If you're going to fabricate the answers to security questions, at least write them down so you can remember them!

Now, let's get back to Boris and Charlie's money. Boris has gained access to Charlie's bank accounts from the comfort of his apartment in Eastern Europe. But, since Charlie's bank isn't going to simply turn over his money to Boris via a wire transfer, Boris has to devise a clever way to physically get his hands on the cash. So Boris put an advertisement on Craigslist or Monster.com, in which he wrote that he was looking for someone who wanted to earn extra income by working as an accounts receivable clerk. The job description stated that an individual would enjoy the comforts of working at home while collecting and reconciling outstanding balances received from several vendors. In return, the accounts receivable clerk would be paid five to ten percent of the money he or she collects. The remaining balance would be sent to

Boris through electronic check or Western Union. Sounds like a dream job for a stay-at-home mom or retiree! Once his new employee was hired, Boris logged in to Charlie's bank account and sent an electronic check to his clerk's newly established account. The employee wired Boris's share via another ACH or Western Union, and Boris collected the stolen cash minutes later. By the time Charlie figured out his money was missing, it was too late to contact the bank or call the police.

I don't care how much you love to fish, you can be sure that the one *not* having fun is the fish dangling at the end of your line. The same is true for phishing. When you're the one stuck on someone else's hook, you'll wish you hadn't fallen for the sparkling bait floating through your email inbox.

CHAPTER 4

Think Before You Click

POST-THANKSGIVING HOLIDAY SHOPPING IS AN AMERICAN phenomenon that I'll never understand. Every year, millions and millions of shoppers line up outside department stores and shopping malls and wait hours to save a few bucks on flat-screen TVs, game consoles, and whatever else is on sale. Shoppers used to wait until Black Friday, the day after Thanksgiving, but now they're even hitting stores on Thursday night. Another new phenomenon is Cyber Monday, the Monday after Thanksgiving weekend, when online retailers have their big holiday shopping sales. Americans spend billions of dollars every year purchasing gifts through e-commerce in a single day.

Do you have any idea what holiday comes next? It's called Bad Guy Tuesday. If you haven't heard of Bad Guy Tuesday, it's because I made it up. But I'm convinced that cybercriminals around the world take Thanksgiving weekend off to rest and relax so they can get ready for the day after Cyber Monday. That morning, they blanket the world with phishing emails that are designed to trick you into clicking a link presumably to Amazon, Best Buy, Target, Walmart, FedEx, or UPS. I think the bad guys probably do it again around December 23, when they send emails informing us that our package delivery has been delayed. How many of us would immediately panic and click the link? If you're like me, the good news is that you probably haven't even started your holiday shopping by December 23!

One of the most important things to remember about phishing is that bad guys are always coming up with new ways to deceive us through emails. It usually involves opening an email, clicking a link, opening an attachment, or having you enter your username and password. And cybercriminals have billions of email addresses that they've stolen in data breaches. In May 2017, there was a massive phishing attack on Google email users. Highly sophisticated malware sent an emailed invitation to users from someone they might have known that asked them to click a link. Once users clicked, the recipients were taken to a legitimate Google sign-in screen, where they were asked to continue to Google Docs. By clicking *yes*, however, the users were actually giving permission to a malicious third-party application that was programmed to steal passwords, emails, and everything else they'd linked to a Google account. The scariest part about this particular worm is that it worked *within* Google's system. When users clicked the link, the malware sent spam messages to the people in the victims' address books, replicating the scenario over and over again. Google said about one million (only one percent) of its email accounts were infected by the Google Docs malware, but that's still a lot of people who were compromised. The Google attack is another reminder that Internet users need to think before they click a link, even if it appears to come from someone they know.

Unfortunately, these types of attacks are nothing new. Bad guys have been targeting Google for years. In 2010, I received an email from one of my wife's friend's Gmail accounts. The woman's name was Brenda and I'd seen her around the neighborhood, but I'd never communicated with her through email. The email contained a message asking for my input, as well as a link to Google Docs. Of course, I live in a world where I investigate bad things on the Internet every day, and an unexpected email asking me to do something was automatically a red flag. I responded to the message with a question, "Did you mean to send this to me? If you didn't, your account has been taken over by a bad guy."

I received a response from Brenda a few minutes later that read, "Oh, Scott, you're being paranoid. I really want your input."

While that comment might satisfy most people, it wasn't a sufficient reply for a cynical FBI agent from New York. In my line of work, I trust nothing that's included in an email until it has been thoroughly verified. I responded once again, "Do you want me to forward this email to my wife, Ann? She is better at these things than I am."

A few minutes later, Brenda responded, "Yes, please send this to Ann." No problem—except that my wife's name isn't Ann! I picked up the phone, called Brenda, and explained what was happening to her Gmail account. At first, she didn't understand the gravity of the situation. But then I sat down with her and explained how the email had been sent to more than three thousand people in her address book. She was employed by a successful multilevel sales organization, and there is no telling how many of her contacts attempted to view the document in Google Docs.

I analyzed the email back at the FBI office, and we discovered that nothing *appeared* to happen when we clicked on the link, which is an everyday occurrence on the Internet. However, the people who clicked the link were unknowingly taken to a webserver in Russia that attempted to infect their computers with malware. We opened the email on a virtual machine in our computer lab to examine it further. A virtual machine is a computer within a computer that runs in a safe, sandboxed environment where malware can't do any damage. When we clicked the link, the malware on the webserver attempted to infect our virtual machine with viruses designed to steal usernames and passwords for any mission-critical account. We then tested the malware against twelve publicly available antivirus products, and eight of them didn't recognize it as a threat. I know you don't want to hear this, but antivirus products are only 30—40 percent effective on their best days. That's because malware writers develop more than one hundred thousand new strains of malware each day. It's basically a race against the bad guys, and antivirus products can only protect against *known* malware. You can't fight what you don't yet know exists, and it's dangerously easy for new strains to go undetected. This type of malware is called a *zero-day exploit* because once it's released into the wild, there's no available cure until antivirus companies write antidotes or signatures to contain it.

I still wonder how many of Brenda's friends clicked the link and had address books, usernames, and passwords stolen. She operated a successful stay-at-home business. She had a following of customers who trusted her, and many of them likely opened any link she sent in an email. When Brenda attempted to log in to her account to see what other damage the bad guys had done, she discovered she no longer had access because they'd changed her password. Her business came to a grinding halt while she contacted Google and tried to regain access. Once your account has been compromised, it isn't easy convincing your email provider that you're the legitimate account holder.

Now, I'm sure there are a couple of folks reading this right now who might say they don't have anything to worry about because they own Apple computers, iPads, or iPhones. A lot of people incorrectly believe that those types of macOS or iOS devices are immune to the bad things I've been talking about. My friend, I hate to be the bearer of bad news, but the belief that Apple products are immune to malware is absolute fiction. In 2011, a malware attack attempted to steal Apple owners' usernames and passwords by sending out an email with the subject line, "Apple update your Billing Information," from a spoofed email address of appleid.apple.com. More recently, in February 2018, a fraudulent pop-up asked Apple users to enter their Apple IDs and passwords. The best advice I can give iOS users is to only enter Apple IDs and passwords within the Settings app or iTunes Store and never in pop-ups.

I had one FBI case involving the owner of a small financial firm who was a long-time iOS user. His name was Rogers, and he received an email from a client with whom he was having a business dispute. The email subject line read, "Please read this important document." There was what appeared to be a PDF document attached to the email. Rogers was curious, so he clicked on the PDF. Instead of seeing a document, Rogers was directed to a webpage that indicated there was a DocuSign document to see. DocuSign is a legitimate online company that facilitates the electronic exchanges of contracts and other sensitive documents. More than two hundred million people around the world have used it. Rogers told me that he thought his client was suing him, so he clicked on the DocuSign document. Unfortunately, Rogers was about to learn about cybercrime the hard way. He was a little leery when he received the document, so he replied to the sender and asked if the communication was legitimate. He didn't realize that bad guys had taken over his client's email account, and a response told Rogers it was indeed for real. When Rogers attempted to open the DocuSign document, he was taken to a webpage that instructed him to enter his Microsoft username and password.

A few hours later, I received an unsolicited email from Rogers with the subject line, "Please read this important document." The email included an attached PDF. At this point, Rogers hadn't shared any details with me, so I quickly picked up the phone and called him. He was panicked after realizing someone else had access to his email account because he'd provided his Microsoft username and password. The bad guys had sent an email to more than one thousand individuals in his address book, many of whom were his clients. Even worse, the criminals deleted all of Rogers' contacts in his address book, so he couldn't send a follow-up email to warn them to delete the original message. The cybercrooks also had access to his OneDrive online storage account, which contained all his client records. And that wasn't all! They were also able to obtain—you guessed it—a file that contained the passwords for each of his bank accounts. Now, do you still feel like you're safe simply because you're using an iOS device? The most important thing to remember is that bad guys want access to your usernames and passwords at any cost, and they are going to use every dirty trick they can to steal them. Your email account is a gold mine, and, once they have access, they're going to use it to trick other people into giving up their usernames and passwords too. Or they'll just install malware on their computers to do it for them.

As I said, antivirus and intrusion detection systems aren't always going to save you, and neither is an Apple computer. That's why you need to completely change your mindset about online security. You need to become a human firewall, questioning every email you receive. If your bank sends you an email about something, pick up the phone and call a local branch. If you receive an email from FedEx or UPS about a delay in shipping and you're not expecting a package, call them. And if you *are* expecting a package, don't click the link and log in to a web portal. If you receive an email with a Facebook or LinkedIn friend request, don't click on the link to log in to the application or website. If your best friend or a family member sends you an email with a link or attachment, think twice before clicking on it. Send them an email first to ask if it's legitimate. I could go on and on with the different scenarios I saw while investigating cybercrime for the FBI.

Because phishing emails are more sophisticated and advanced than ever before, it's much easier to be tricked into clicking. Some of them are so good, I'm afraid that even I might even fall for it one day. So, repeat after me: *I will think before clicking on emails and will become a human firewall.* Repeating that step one thousand times is the first step to being safe online.

HOW TO AVOID BECOMING A VICTIM

🔒 Become a human firewall and examine every email you receive. Realize that bad guys want to use your email account as a weapon.

🔒 Understand that bad guys desperately want you to click a link or open an attachment in an email. Unless you've thoroughly validated its authenticity, don't click on it!

🔒 Look at the time an email was sent. If it was sent at 2:30 A.M. and you know that person never sends email that late, don't open it before verifying it.

🔒 Check the other recipients of the email. If an email was sent to a large group of people, it usually means the account was compromised and an automated program sent the message.

🔒 If you receive an email with an urgent message from your bank, credit card company, utility company, FedEx, UPS, Amazon, eBay, Facebook, LinkedIn, Instagram, or any other financial institution or social media application, don't open it or click on a link! Log in to the actual account manually through a browser or application to check if there's a legitimate issue.

🔒 Make a list of important telephone numbers, such as your bank and credit card companies, and call the numbers you have instead of the ones included in suspicious emails.

🔒 If you receive an email containing a friend request from social media, do not click on the link in the message to log in to the account. Bad guys love to use social media friend requests to target victims. If I receive a connection request from LinkedIn, I automatically delete the email and then log in to the actual LinkedIn application to see if it's a legitimate request.

🔒 This is very important: Do not store your usernames and passwords for financial institutions, credit card companies, utilities, email, and social media on OneDrive, Dropbox, Google Drive, or iCloud. Write them down on a sheet of paper and store the physical copy somewhere safe.

CHAPTER 5

Mobile Device Safety

I'VE TALKED ABOUT THE IMPORTANCE OF THINKING BEFORE you click on email, but there are other ways cybercriminals will try to trick you. My sister, Bonni, is the principal of an elementary school in Long Island, New York, and she is an understandably busy person. Recently, she received a text message from her bank, informing her that her checking account was overdrawn because of a $2,000 transaction. The text from the bank instructed her to click a link that would take her to the bank's website for an important message. If she didn't address the problem immediately, the text message said, she'd be charged a hefty overdraft fee.

Of course, being the sister of an FBI agent who investigates cyber-crime, Bonni had heard me go on and on about the importance of thinking before you click on an email. But this was a text message sent to her cell phone, and she was pretty sure she'd provided the bank with her number in case they needed to contact her. Fortunately, she was driving by her branch when she received the text, so she stopped and talked to a representative. The bank employee checked her account and told her there wasn't a problem and that the text message was actually a scam.

As cybersecurity continues to evolve, cybercriminals create new *and* not-so-new methods to persuade people to divulge their usernames and passwords. One way is called smishing, which is short for SMS (short message service) phishing. Smishing is another tool cybercriminals use to access personally identifiable information and steal identities, gain access to your accounts, or help themselves to your money and credit by infecting your smartphone through texts or SMS messaging. Smishing is also used to spread viruses that contain keyloggers. As we've seen, these are programs that hide in the background, waiting to steal your credentials or install ransomware on your phone, making it useless unless you pay the crook's extortion demands.

Smishing is a growing threat in the world of online security. One big reason is that nearly every U.S. adult uses some type of cell phone, and most of them are using smartphones. According to a 2018 Pew Research Center study, 95 percent of U.S. adults own a cell phone and 77 percent own smartphones (up from 35 percent in a 2011 study). And now, more and more Americans are relying solely on their smartphones to access the Internet. According to the Pew Research Center study, one in five American adults is a smartphone-only Internet user who does not have traditional broadband Internet service at home. In fact, 63 percent of total Internet visits in 2017 were from mobile devices (up from 57 percent the previous year), according to a study by SimilarWeb—and that number is expected to grow every year. Cybercriminals have taken notice of that trend, and they've altered their arsenals to attack our cell phones and smartphones, whether it's by smishing, spoofing mobile sites, fraudulent promotional offers, or fake login landing pages. Cybercriminals like sending viruses and malware to cell phones because the screens are smaller and users are less likely to closely examine webpages and emails.

As people have become more reliant on their smartphones (and more suspicious of emails and thus less likely to click on links or attachments), the bad guys are relying more and more on text messages to do their dirty work. Because smishing has been less prevalent in the past, people are less suspicious of a text message from their bank or close friends. For whatever reason, people seem to trust a text message more than an email, and they feel less vulnerable when using their smartphones. Plus, massive data breaches in the recent past have given cybercriminals access to millions of cell phone numbers, which have been packaged and sold on the dark web. In late 2016, the ride-sharing service provider Uber announced that a data breach had affected about fifty-seven million customers, revealing their names, email addresses, and phone numbers. Uber later admitted to keeping the breach secret for a year and paying the hackers $100,000 in ransom money. In another data breach, personal data belonging to about 1.5 million members of E-Sports Entertainment Association League was leaked online by hackers after the company refused to pay a ransom. Now it's probably easy to understand how cybercriminals might have your cell phone number.

Text messages and mobile emails aren't the only weapons for cyber-attacks. According to Wandera's "Mobile Data Report" in July 2017, only 19 percent of mobile attacks originated through mobile emails. The majority—81 percent—came through mobile applications and websites.

It also may surprise you that Wandera's data showed 63 percent of the phones attacked had iOS operating systems (remember what I said about Apple products?) and 37 percent were Android devices.

If my sister had clicked on the link included in the text message, she would have been taken to a website that looked like her bank's actual website. She would have been instructed to enter her username and password, and then it would have been game over. The thieves would have wiped out the money in her checking and savings accounts. Fortunately, she outsmarted them.

Bonni asked me how the bad guys obtained her phone number and knew where she banked. I explained they were able to do it because her consumer habits are like most of ours. First, we provide our cell phone numbers when we sign up for banking and finance, e-commerce, utilities, and even social media services. Somewhere along the way, bad guys probably hacked into one of those sites and stole the numbers.

In some cases, cybercriminals will even randomly text numbers in certain area codes, hoping to win the lottery by duping a couple of unsuspecting victims. Bonni lives in Long Island, New York, which is located in the 516 area code. She banks with Chase Bank, which is quite popular in that area. The cybercrooks might have taken a shotgun approach and simply sent hundreds of thousands of text messages to numbers in the 516 area code. Unfortunately, they have automated ways of doing it that make crime easy and efficient nowadays. Think about it: If the bad guys sent out one hundred thousand text messages and only one hundred of the recipients actually did their banking at Chase, how many of them would fall for the scam, click on the link, and provide their credentials? It would probably only be a handful. But the criminals might only need *one person* to respond to make it worth their time and effort, depending on how much money they steal.

Sometimes, attackers will send a text message asking you to call a bank's phone number, which is only an attempt to further persuade you to divulge your personal information. If you receive such a text message, call the bank using a number from your statements or one you've written down. Never call the number included in the text message. You'd probably be talking to some guy sitting on a couch in Eastern Europe or Southeast Asia.

Unfortunately, it is becoming difficult for law enforcement to stop smishing. I received dozens of calls from banks when I worked for the FBI informing me that cybercriminals were sending these types of text messages to their customers. The banks provided me with a list of phone numbers from which the smishing messages originated, and they expected me to track the bad guys down.

Let me explain why it's so difficult. In the old days, you had to have a physical address to have a hardline phone in your home. Today, through Google, Skype, and other online phone providers, you can obtain free *voice over Internet protocol* (VOIP) numbers that enable you to call a phone through your computer. Through free VOIP numbers, it's easy for criminals to send out smishing messages, and it's extremely difficult for law enforcement to trace those numbers. Even when law enforcement goes through the long and arduous process of sending a subpoena to an Internet provider, the originating Internet protocol (IP) address usually resides in a foreign country. If we're fortunate to shut one down, the cybercriminal simply moves to another IP address. Stopping them is like playing a game of Whack-a-Mole; you knock one down and another pops up. The hard truth is we cannot stop the bad guys from sending text messages with links. It's impossible. What we *can* do is teach people how to react and how not to react. Whenever possible, I've encouraged people in the financial sector to educate their customers on the different types of smishing scams. If they were doing their jobs effectively, I probably wouldn't have needed to write this book.

The episode with my sister and her cell phone made me think about my own cell number, which is also my work phone. I tell people it's the best way to reach me. I decided to conduct a test and searched for my cell phone number on Google. Much to my surprise, I saw it listed on a website. I figured it was there because I'd previously provided it to a company as my contact number, and it was either sold without my knowledge or stolen through a data breach. I'm not going to lie: what I discovered was absolutely frightening. The website that had my cell phone number was strange-looking. When I clicked on that link, I was taken to a different webpage that included my name, date of birth, home address, work address, wife's and mother's names and dates of birth, and every phone number and physical address I've had for the past twenty years. The website claims to be a data aggregator; it crawls the Internet specifically searching for personal information of people living in the U.S. It combines the best social networking information with all publicly available information for everyone over the age of eighteen. The site boasts of having one of the largest public records repositories on the Internet (it had information for nearly two hundred million people and more than eighteen million companies in 2018), and I'm sure it's expanding rapidly every day.

What was frightening about this particular site is that its point of contact was listed as someone in Africa. I didn't have a good feeling about the entire situation. It comes down to a fundamental question: do we have an expectation of privacy on the Internet? Or should we assume there's somebody sitting in Africa collecting all our personal information and probably selling it to anyone who will pay? In the old days, you simply needed to have an unlisted phone number and that alone made it difficult for someone to find you. Today, everything about you is online, and those details are being aggregated and sold. Privacy has gone out the window! And, if this information gets into the hands of bad guys, the chances of you becoming a victim are extremely high.

HOW TO AVOID BECOMING A VICTIM

🔒 Be aware of smishing. You need to become a human firewall when it comes to text messaging.

🔒 Use strong passwords or fingerprint/biometric features to secure your cell phone. Doing so will protect your phone if it's lost or stolen.

🔒 Disable Wi-Fi or Bluetooth when you're not using it. Free public Wi-Fi service in public places like airports, shopping malls, and sporting venues typically aren't secure. Never log on to financial or email accounts while using public Wi-Fi.

🔒 Don't click on a link included in a text message until you have thoroughly vetted its legitimacy. It is easy for bad guys to send text messages to a massive number of recipients through automated means. If you don't recognize the phone number that sent you the message, don't click the link!

🔒 Remember that clicking a link in a text message can cause ransomware or a virus to be installed on your smartphone. Computers aren't the only devices affected by viruses, worms, and other cybercrime tools.

🔒 Keep your mobile phone and apps updated for the latest security software. Your mobile devices are just as vulnerable as your laptops and desktop computers. Having the latest security software, operating systems, web browsers, and apps are the best defenses against online threats.

🔒 Ignore text messages from numbers you don't know. Your cell phone number might be in the hands of someone who shouldn't have it.

🔒 If you receive a suspicious text message from a familiar number, call that person at the number in your contacts and ask if the message is legitimate.

🔒 If you receive a text message from a number such as 5000, it's a sign that the message is actually just an email sent to your phone. Don't click the link!

🔒 Don't download any mobile apps that don't come directly from a trusted app store like Apple's App Store or Google's Play Store. Cybercriminals assemble cheaper alternatives to games and other apps, which are designed to harvest your credentials and personal information.

🔒 Consider installing a full-service Internet security suite on your mobile device that will encrypt any communication between your phone and the Internet. It's better to be safe than sorry.

CHAPTER 6

Password Safety

I LIKE TO JOKE THAT NO ONE ON THE PLANET HAS BEEN THE victim of more data breaches than I have. The Office of Personnel Management, Anthem Healthcare, Target, The Home Depot, Sony, P.F. Chang's, J.P. Morgan, Marriott, and Equifax have all lost my personal information. In my opinion, however, each of those incidents wasn't nearly as bad as what I consider the granddaddy of all breaches—Yahoo!. When I bring up the Yahoo! breach of 2013 during my presentations, someone in the audience will undoubtedly challenge me. They'll argue that since no personally identifiable information—such as dates of birth, addresses, or Social Security numbers—was compromised, it wasn't really a big deal.

But Yahoo! and its parent company, Verizon, disclosed in October 2017 that every single customer account that Yahoo! had at the time was affected by the data breach. That's more than three billion accounts, including email, Tumblr, Fantasy, and Flickr. It's also three times more than Yahoo! initially reported as being compromised in 2016. Cybercriminals walked away with more than three billion usernames, passwords, and answers to security questions. Yahoo! officials told users that a sophisticated foreign adversary pulled off the largest data breach in history, and then it reluctantly instructed its users to change their usernames and passwords. Shockingly, it wasn't a mandatory change, and there's no good way to determine how many people actually did it.

Remember, Yahoo! just isn't Yahoo!. At the time, the company also included AT&T and BellSouth, along with other smaller Internet providers. The bad guys gained access to billions of email accounts, and then they were able to turn them into weapons by sending out billions of spear-phishing emails. And, once they gained access to someone's email account, they were able to discover the inner workings of that person's life—including financial records, social media accounts, sensitive work documents, and who knows what else.

Here's where it starts to get really bad. Let's say one billion of those three billion Yahoo! users owned an iPhone, iPad, or iMac desktop computer. That's 33 percent of the users; some analysts have estimated it might be closer to 50 percent or more. Let's assume, for argument's sake, that only 1 percent of the Yahoo! victims owned some sort of Apple device. One percent of three billion is still thirty million users. There's a good chance many of the Yahoo! victims were using the same usernames and passwords for their iCloud accounts. What kind of damage can a cybercriminal do if he gains access to your iCloud account? He can wreak havoc by changing the username and password and locking you out of your account. He can hold your account hostage and demand thousands of dollars to release it. Many people are using cloud accounts to back up intimate details of their lives, so now the bad guys have access to everything—photos, email, movies, music, documents, calendars, and a lot more.

You may have heard about the targeted attack on Apple usernames, passwords, and security questions in September 2014. Hackers released intimate photos of several celebrities, including actress Jennifer Lawrence and model Kate Upton. The photos were released to the world, but the celebrities didn't have anyone to sue because anonymous hackers committed the crime. They were helpless in trying to stop the photos from being revealed.

While some of the celebrities in the Apple hack were obviously embarrassed and might have been forced to have uncomfortable conversations with their parents, less-famous Yahoo! victims suffered greater financial damage. Cybercriminals have written scripts—simple automated programs—that can compare Yahoo! usernames and passwords with thousands of popular websites, such as banks, social media, e-commerce, and so on. If you use the same username and password for your Yahoo! account that you do for your iCloud account, there's a good chance it's going to be the same login credentials you also use for Amazon, eBay, American Express, and bank accounts. The thieves will scrutinize your emails to determine where you do business and attempt to gain access to *all* those accounts. Their automated programs allow them to gain access without even having to manually enter usernames and passwords. Even if they're successful only 1 percent of the time, it's still a lucrative business when you're talking about information from three billion Yahoo! accounts.

During a 2017 speech at the Black Hat USA conference in Las Vegas, Facebook chief security officer Alex Stamos explained to the audience why password reuse is one of the largest online dangers. Stamos told the crowd, "[The] vast majority of harm comes from the simple problems that are difficult to solve, such as the rampant reuse of passwords. When people use one password for their bank, social media, their email, and a gambling site, the gambling site may get broken into and then those credentials will be sold on the black market. Now dozens of attackers will fight to be the first one to take over that person's digital identity."

I can't stress enough the importance of having separate and strong passwords for mission-critical accounts. Mission-critical accounts are email, social media, cell phones, banking, and e-commerce. Think of anything you don't want criminals to gain access to, and this even includes alarm systems, garage door openers, and security cameras. I'll never forget one of the cybercrime cases I investigated while working for the Federal Bureau of Investigation. The case involved a woman named Ellen who was the mother of four children and a successful entrepreneur with a massive social media following. Unfortunately, Ellen was like most other people when it came to online security. She used simple passwords and reused them for most of her online accounts. A bad guy in Central Asia gained access to Ellen's Facebook account because her password was a combination of one of her children's names and the year the child was born. He probably found that information on her publicly available Facebook page in a matter of minutes.

Once the cybercriminal had access to Ellen's Facebook account, he discovered that she used an iCloud email account. It didn't take him long to figure out that her login credentials for her iCloud email were the same as what she used on Facebook. So, he logged into her email account and read her email. The first thing he did was log in to the Apple Store, order ten new iPad minis, and have them delivered to Central Asia. Fortunately for him, Ellen had saved her credit card information in her Apple account. By examining Ellen's email, this crook was able to identify about ten different mission-critical accounts. He changed the usernames and passwords for each of them and locked her out of her own accounts. Then he sent Ellen a ransom email, telling her to send him money to regain access. When Ellen received the email, she was furious and sent him a nasty reply. He responded by deleting the contents of Ellen's iCloud account, which contained keepsake family photographs and multiple files of her uncompleted work. After that, he started targeting several of Ellen's friends and followers, wreaking havoc on their lives, as well. It took Ellen weeks to regain control of her accounts. It was like the bad guy was always one step ahead of her. He even left a forwarding rule in Ellen's email account that allowed him to receive a copy of every email sent to her. Each time Ellen received an email with a temporary password, he intercepted the email. I've seen this technique used in dozens of situations, and it's very difficult to stop.

Through our criminal investigation, we tracked down the person responsible for Ellen's nightmare. We discovered it was a twenty-one-year-old man from Central Asia who was working alone. He had also gained access to email accounts belonging to about a half-dozen of Ellen's friends and followers, causing a lot of trouble for them, as well.

Fortunately, FBI agents are assigned overseas to help protect American citizens at home. They build relationships with foreign governments, law enforcement, intelligence agencies, and security services around the world, promoting a prompt and continuous exchange of information. There are sixty-four legal attaché offices—commonly known as legats—and more than a dozen smaller sub-offices in key cities around the world that provide coverage in more than two hundred countries, territories, and islands. Each office is established through mutual agreements with host countries and is located in the U.S. embassy or consulate in that country.

Once we identified the cybercriminal in Ellen's case, I established contact with an FBI colleague who was located in the Central Asian country where the thief lived. Unfortunately, the host government there didn't have a formal treaty with the U.S. So, even if we had brought criminal charges against the man who victimized Ellen, we couldn't have extradited him back to the U.S. However, the man *could* have been prosecuted for his crimes in his native country. My colleague asked me to send him the facts of the case and what we knew so the host government could conduct its own investigation. A few weeks later, ISIS attacked their country, and prosecuting a twenty-one-year-old man who was hacking a U.S. citizen was no longer a priority. Remember what I told you about not getting your stuff back and the bad guys not going to jail? Ellen never recovered her data that was erased, and we weren't able to put the man in jail. The entire situation might have been prevented if she hadn't used the same username and password for multiple online platforms.

There are hundreds of other similar horror stories involving password reuse that I could tell you about, and there's one particular incident I haven't been able to forget since retiring from the FBI. The case involved the chief financial officer of a large organization, a man who was quite active on Facebook. Unfortunately, he wasn't careful when using social media, and he even listed his work email address on his Facebook page. Somehow, a bad guy gained access to his Facebook account. Once the cybercriminal gained access to the CFO's Facebook page, he was also able to access the man's work email. He browsed through the executive's emails and, within a few hours, had a good understanding of how his employer operated. The criminal spoofed an email from the chief financial officer to the company's controller, instructing her to pay an invoice for several thousand dollars. The controller, believing the email was legitimately from the CFO, followed his instructions and paid the invoice. Somewhere in West Africa, a cybercriminal enjoyed a very large payday for very little work. It could have been prevented if the CFO used different usernames and passwords for his Facebook account and work email.

In August 2018, the FBI revealed another growing online threat, in which criminals were gaining access to employees' work login credentials, either through phishing emails, spoof PDFs, telephone conversations, or other unlawful means. The bad actors would then gain access to payroll portals, changing bank account numbers and diverting direct deposits to other bank accounts or prepaid bank cards they controlled. In many cases, fraudulent payroll deposits were transferred from multiple victims' accounts. The Bureau identified approximately seventeen such cases in 2017 and forty-seven in 2018, with losses totaling approximately $1 million. The FBI said criminals were targeting universities, local school districts, healthcare, and commercial airlines.

Here's the bottom line: **Having the same username and password for multiple online platforms is a recipe for disaster.** This only makes it easier for cybercriminals to gain access to your email and bank accounts, which can cause financial ruin not only for you, but also for your employer, family, and friends.

HOW TO AVOID BECOMING A VICTIM

🔒 Do not use the same username and password for mission-critical accounts. This includes email, social media, cell phones, banking, and e-commerce.

🔒 Don't use Yahoo! for email. The company was the subject of two massive data breaches that resulted in more than three billion accounts being compromised. Two Russian spies were indicted for the smaller of the two hacks; it's still unclear who the architect was of the larger one. I'm sorry, but I don't trust Yahoo! to protect your online personal identity.

🔒 Ensure that your login credentials used for payroll purposes differ from those used for other online platforms. If a bad guy obtains your payroll information, he'll be collecting your hard-earned money.

🔒 If you need to write down passwords to remember them, encrypt them in a way that is easy for you to remember but makes them inde-cipherable by anyone else. We'll talk more about this in the following chapter.

🔒 Use a different password for every website. If you have only one password, it's too easy for a criminal to break in to gain access to everything.

🔒 Don't recycle passwords, such as bigbomber1, bigbomber2, bigbomber3. Make sure your passwords are unique.

🔒 Never disclose your username and passwords to someone else, even if it's a family member or close friend. If you believe someone else knows your login credentials, change them immediately. While a friend or family member probably won't want to do you harm, someone who steals from them might gain access to your credentials.

CHAPTER 7

Strong Passwords

WHETHER WE LIKE THEM OR NOT, PASSWORDS HAVE BECOME a part of our everyday lives. We need them to unlock our cell phones and computers, access cash from ATMs, and stream movies from Netflix. The average American is going to have somewhere between ten to twenty mission-critical accounts at various points in his or her life, whether they're email, banking websites, social media, or credit cards. You need a *unique* password for every one of them. When I make this comment during my presentations, most people in the audience give me a look that says, *That's too hard.* If you think that's difficult, just wait until I tell you what a good password is.

Before we get into how to set up a strong, secure password, let's discuss what a bad password would be. My son Aidan was born in 2002 and his brother Quinn came along in 2005. Do you think I've ever used the passwords "Aidan2002" and "Quinn2005"? I have. They were easy to remember and at least I was using two passwords instead of one. Then I came up with a third password that nobody could possibly ever guess; it included my initials, my wife's initials, and the date of our anniversary. As someone who used three passwords for everything, I'm guessing I was probably doing better than 95 percent of the U.S. population—but it still wasn't nearly enough to prevent cybercriminals from hacking my accounts. Think about your passwords for a second. How many passwords do you use for multiple platforms? I'm guessing they're all probably the same (or a slight variation of each other), and I bet they're related to significant things in your life, such as your children, birthdays, anniversaries, pets, or hometown. I hate to tell you this, but those are absolutely terrible passwords, and I was as guilty as anyone of using them.

In my opinion, a good password is typically at least twelve characters in length and must contain an upper- and lowercase letter, numbers, and at least one special character. If you want a really *great* password, make it fifteen characters. And, to make it even more unique, a password shouldn't contain any words that you can find in a dictionary. Now, many members of the techie community might argue that twelve characters isn't enough and that strong passwords should be fifteen, twenty, or even twenty-five characters long because of threats like brute-force attacks (trial-and-error tools used by criminals that use automated software to generate a massive of number of consecutive guesses) and dictionary attacks (an automated attack that uses—you guessed it—every word in the dictionary). There is quite a bit of debate about password length and password complexity, but I'm only trying to come up with something stronger than "Aidan2002" and "Quinn2005."

Normally, when I tell people they need ten to twenty unique passwords that are at least twelve characters in length, they'll say something like, "This guy is crazy. I can't do that. I'm not even going to try. There's no way I'm going to remember every one of them." Then, in my best Tony Robbins or Joel Osteen voice, I'll explain to them that it's only going to take me five minutes to teach them a system that will change their passwords and help remember them. I've even taught my system at retirement homes, and each of the lovely men and women were able to do it. It's not that hard.

First, let's define our objective. We have identified our mission-critical accounts, and now we need to devise separate passwords for each one. Each password needs to be twelve characters in length, contain upper- and lowercase letters, and should also have numbers and at least one special character. We're also not going to use words that are included in the dictionary. It might sound difficult, but I'm positive you'll be surprised how easy it really is.

The first thing you have to do is decide your favorite numbers and special characters, and don't share them with anyone—not even your husband or wife, children, roommates, or best friends. Let's call this the top-secret combination. For example, let's say my top-secret combo is %7. Now come up with your top-secret combo and store it in your brain because you're going to use this combination in each of your passwords.

Next, you're going to come up with something to replace the traditional passwords, which might be your children's names, pets' names, high school mascot, or favorite vacation spot. It's too easy for cybercriminals to find those things on social media and other places online. Instead, you should think of a simple passphrase that's easy to remember. Let's start the process by figuring out how the passphrase is related to the specific accounts. For instance, the passphrase for my Amazon account might be, "I hate to shop at Amazon very much." If that offends you, then use my wife's passphrase: "I love to shop at Amazon very much." I use this example in the majority of my presentations, and each time I usually have the room laughing. If I were a stand-up comic, it would be my go-to line.

Now it's time to create a password using the sentence we just came up with. We are going to start by putting the top-secret combo in front, and then we are going to reverse the order of the characters when we put them at the end. So, it's going to start out as:

%7_____7%

Next, we're going to put the first letter of our phrase into the password field. Remember that our phrase for Amazon is, "I love to shop at Amazon very much." I prefer passphrases that use the letter "I" because I can substitute the number "1" (one) for "I."

%71_____7%

Now, we'll use our verb in the passphrase, which in this case is the letter "l" for love.

%71l_____7%

The word "to" is also one of my favorites, because it can be substituted with the number "2" (two).

%71l2_____7%

The next word in the passphrase is shop, so we use the letter "s."

%7112s_____7%

Using the word "at" is another one of my favorites because you can use the symbol "@" as a substitute.

%7112s@_____7%

As we finish up our password, we place the first letters of the rest of the words in our passphrase, which in this case are "a" for Amazon, "v" for very, and "m" for much. So, the password for my Amazon account would be:

%7112s@avm7%

Now, you might be asking yourself: what about the capital letter? To make it easy, it's going to be the first letter of the first word or last word in the passphrase. Since we substituted the number 1 for I, let's go with the last word in this example:

%7112s@avM7%

If you look closely at this password, the first thing that probably comes to mind is, *How in the world does this guy expect me to remember such a long and ugly-looking password?* Remember, I don't need you to remember the password. I only need you to remember your special symbol, number combination, and the passphrase, "I love to shop at Amazon very much." You will come up with your own passphrases; this is only an example.

We should come up with a couple of other passwords just to make sure you understand the concept. I want you to come up with something that's completely original. The phrase should be at least eight words long; that plus your special symbol and number at the beginning and end of your password will get you to twelve characters. If you *really* want to be safe, make your phrase eleven words long, which will give you a fifteen-character password. You'll probably find yourself using filler words, which is fine. Don't be afraid to play around and be creative. Come up with phrases such as:

I can never ever remember my Gmail password =
%71cnermgP7%

I love my First Trust Bank very much =
%71lmftbvM7%

See how these passwords, like the Amazon example, are directly tied to specific site? In this case, Gmail and First Trust Bank respectively. But you can also use this system to come up with generic passwords for anything else. Here are a few other phrases and the corresponding passwords:

I love to eat gyros with tahini sauce at Nick's =
%71l2egwts@N7%

My first bank account was at Lincoln Savings Bank =
%7m1stbaw@lsB7%

I love to go to ski at Mount Snow Vermont =
%71l2g2s@msV7%

I don't trust the stock market as means to investment =
%71dttsmam2l7%

I loved my job as a delivery boy at Key Foods Supermarket = %71Imjaadb@kfS7%

I recently made a presentation to a group of church administrators. One of the audience members approached me afterwards and wanted some ideas about creating passphrases for her QuickBooks, payroll, banking, and email accounts. I rattled off the following passphrases:

"I enjoy QuickBooks more than the ledger book."

"Paying our employees puts food on their kitchen table."

"We love to bank at our favorite bank."

I challenge you to change every one of your passwords, and it shouldn't require more than twenty minutes to change the passwords for your ten to twenty mission-critical accounts. After you've changed your passwords, you might be wondering how you're going to remember them. In the beginning, you need to do what you've been told not to do: write them down. Not your passwords, but your passphrases. Don't do what my CPA wife did. She changed all our passwords and put them on a Microsoft Excel spreadsheet (without a password protecting the file) and then saved the file to the home screen of her computer. In the South, they'd say, "Bless her heart." In New York, though, we say, "What the [expletive]?" What should my wife have done? She should have used the same format, but instead of writing down the passwords, she should have only saved the written passphrases without her secret combination of a special character and number. If a cybercriminal somehow found our list of passphrases, the only thing he would have figured out is that I have deep-rooted issues, such as really loving some things and absolutely hating others.

Here's another important note: I would find a safe place to store the passphrases. Don't store them on a computer like my wife did. I have them written down on a yellow sticky note in one of my least favorite books in my bookcase. The day will undoubtedly come when I forget my Amazon password; when that happens, I'll find the book with a yellow sticky note that says, "I hate to shop at Amazon very much." That's all I'll need to jog my memory. Find somewhere similar, whether it's inside a book or CD case, behind a picture frame or clock on the wall, or even inside a shoebox in the closet. However—and this is important—you must never keep your top-secret combination near your passphrases. You have to keep that secret inside your head, where no one else can find it.

Isn't that easy to remember? It's not a crazy, overly nerdy approach, but I'm betting it's better than what you're doing, and it's not nearly as difficult as it might have sounded in the beginning. Is this system for building passwords foolproof? No, but it's going to be much more difficult for a bad guy to figure out your passwords. Is this scientific? No. But is it better than "Aidan2002" or "Quinn2005"? Yes, it is.

HOW TO AVOID BECOMING A VICTIM

🔒 Never give out your passwords to anyone, including your family and friends.

🔒 Strong passwords need to be at least twelve characters in length, or even fifteen, twenty, or twenty-five characters if you really want them to be effective. They need to include upper- and lowercase letters, numbers, and at least one special character.

🔒 Don't use words found in the dictionary or personal information like dates, names, and addresses that might be easy to find online.

🔒 Use the same secret combination of a special symbol and number in all your passwords. Use it at the start of the password and then in reverse order at the end. Never share your secret combination with anyone.

🔒 Use a passphrase to devise your passwords. A passphrase contains seemingly random words strung together. Make sure it's something you can remember but others can't guess. Avoid using familiar phrases or famous quotes that others might know.

🔒 Become creative when creating your passphrases. Substitute the number "1" for the letter "l," use the symbol @ for the word "at," and use the number "2" for the word "to." You can also use a dollar sign ("$") instead of an "S."

🔒 Write down the passphrases and keep them in a safe place only you know. Don't store your secret combination of a number and special character with your passphrases. You'll have to remember that combo in your head.

🔒 Don't enter your passwords on devices you don't own. If you're using a public computer at a library, Internet café, or hotel, avoid using your passwords for email, social media, and other mission-critical accounts. Those computers should only be used for anonymous Internet browsing because the networks probably aren't safe.

CHAPTER 8

Two-Factor Authentication

LET'S REVIEW A COUPLE OF IMPORTANT STEPS THAT WILL help prevent you from becoming a cybercrime victim. First, you should by now be saying over and over again, "I will think before I click." When you receive an email from a bank, credit card company, eBay, Amazon, Federal Express, or anybody else who asks you to click on a link, you're going to stop, think, and then make a phone call to determine whether the email or text message containing the link is legitimate.

Second, you're no longer going to have the same password for multiple platforms. And surely you've already identified your mission-critical accounts, such as email, social media, cell phone, banking, and e-commerce. Those are the platforms that require the type of passphrases we discussed in the previous chapter. I showed you how easy it is to create and remember passphrases that consist of twelve characters, with upper- and lowercase letters, numbers, and at least one special symbol. Hopefully, you've written down your pass- phrases and put them in a safe place, and you have *not* written down your top-secret combination of a number and special character. Now that you've done enough to help you sleep a little better at night, we have another important security technique to implement.

A woman approached me with a confident smile after one of my recent seminars and told me she'd been using multiple passphrases for years. She was using a lyric from one of her favorite songs as her pass- phrase, which consisted of twenty characters. I congratulated her and told her it was a great start, but then I asked her what would happen if I were somehow able to get my hands on her passphrase for her bank account. I told her I would be able to log in to her account and steal her money. You can do everything correctly—not click on suspicious links and not use the same password for everything—and yet still become a victim. That sounds really depressing, doesn't it?

Well, fortunately, I'm going to tell you how to take the next step in keeping yourself safe and making it even more difficult for cybercriminals to make you a victim. It's not a well-kept secret and it's not going to cost you a penny to implement. Before I share this technique, though, let's go back to the basics. If a bad guy steals your password, he is going to have access to all your personal information. And, no matter what you do, there is a good chance he's going to be able to steal your money. What if I told you that it might not matter if he steals your password? Doesn't that sound like a much better scenario? There's an additional security measure that makes your passwords obsolete—even if a cybercriminal steals them.

In the past few years, I've probably done more than two hundred cybersecurity threat briefings, including presentations to civic groups, students, corporations, and churches. During each of my presentations, I asked the audience two simple questions. The first one might sound a little silly, but humor me for a second. Here's the question: Is there anyone in the audience who doesn't use email to communicate; doesn't use social media platforms such as LinkedIn, Facebook, Twitter, or Instagram to connect with others; doesn't use online banking or e-commerce to shop; and doesn't store information on a cloud platform? (A cloud platform stores data on the Internet through a cloud-computing provider such as Google Drive, Dropbox, or iCloud. They manage and operate data storage as a service, and millions of people use them to back up their contacts, email, documents, photos, music, and everything else. With cloud storage, you don't have to purchase a storage device and can add or remove capacity on demand.) Unless you're an Eskimo or Amish farmer, you're probably using one or all of the platforms I mentioned every day.

Now, the next question is even more important: do you use multi-factor authentication (MFA) or two-factor authentication (2FA) to access your platform? I always get a couple of confused looks from people in the audience when I ask this question. MFA and 2FA are pretty simple concepts—they involve more than a single password. Think of it this way: if I am able to log in to your Gmail account by simply stealing your password, then you're not using MFA or 2FA. Multi-factor and two-factor authentication means something more than a password is required to access an account. It's an extra layer of cybersecurity that only the user knows or possesses, like a piece of information such as a passcode, pin, or six-digit number that you use *in addition* to your password. When you attempt to log in to an account, the six-digit number is typically provided to you in either a text message to your cell phone, through an application on your smartphone, or by a hard token on a small device like a fob or thumb drive. Advanced biometric-based MFA even replaces traditional passcodes and token-based systems with your fingerprint, facial or voice recognition, iris scans, and other biometics. It's the wave of the future, and it's extremely cool.

If you've never heard of MFA or 2FA, then today is your lucky day because I'm about to explain how easy it is to install them on your platforms. First, though, let me highlight a couple of scary cybercrime statistics to emphasize the importance of two-factor authentication. As you've probably figured out by now, cybercrime is big business around the world; annual economic losses from data breaches are in the trillions of dollars. I told you earlier that analysts predict cybercrime losses will reach $6 trillion by 2020! That's more money than I can wrap my head around, but I'm afraid it's probably accurate. I witnessed hundreds, if not thousands, of cybercrime cases while working for the FBI in Nashville, and I would estimate that victims in those cases probably lost in excess of $100 million. And those are only the cases that were actually reported to the FBI and that I personally helped investigate.

If the victims in my cases had used MFA or 2FA on their personal platforms, many of them wouldn't have been victims of cybercrime. I cringe every time I make that statement because I know it's true and many of the crimes could have been prevented. I worked with a lot of large corporations that were victimized, and they were big enough to survive heavy financial losses. But I can't tell you how often I worked with small businesses, nonprofit organizations, schools, or retirees who lost tens thousands of dollars or more to cybercriminals. In many cases, the victims' lives were ruined. I witnessed small businesses go out of business and retirees lose their entire life savings. They are tragic stories that will haunt me for the rest of my life.

After witnessing the carnage that comes with cybercrime, some of the most important advice I now give to family members and friends—and what I'm going to say to you now—is that you should only use an email provider that offers two-factor authentication. With that added layer of security, a cybercriminal would need your passphrase *and* the security code that's on your mobile device to break into your account. Gmail, Outlook, and iCloud each offer 2FA. The website www.twofactorauth.org is an excellent resource that identifies the platforms that have 2FA and those that don't. One of the big questions I get from people is, "What if my email platform doesn't offer two-factor authentication?" Easy: find one that does. A person once told me that he had a "very cool" email address on a provider that didn't offer 2FA and he didn't want to give it up. I told him to do whatever he wanted, but I wouldn't be opening any emails from him!

In the past, most email platforms offered 2FA through SMS; they'd send you a six-digit verification code via a text message when you attempted to log in to your email from a computer or other device. Well, cybercriminals figured out devious ways to clone cell phones, intercept SMS messages, and hijack accounts simply by calling unsuspecting cellular carriers. Two-factor authentication through SMS is better than doing nothing at all, but token-based 2FA and app-based 2FA are much better alternatives nowadays. If you want to add yet another layer of security, download a password authenticator on your mobile device. Google, Microsoft, and Apple offer such apps through Google Play and the App Store, and there are other options available, such as Authy, LastPass Authenticator, and 1Password. I personally use Duo Mobile, which is free and works across a lot of platforms. These apps, available on both iOS and Android devices, generate random two-step verification codes on your phone—even if it's not connected to the Internet. If you don't have Google Authenticator or another authenticator app, the Gmail verification codes can still be sent to your phone via text messages. But the authenticator apps use algorithms to generate the codes on your phone, making it even safer. You can also transfer the authenticator apps to a new phone if your old device is lost or damaged or if you've replaced it with the latest model.

I have a Gmail account that I use for personal correspondence. Google has an incredibly easy process to utilize 2FA to help me stay safe, and it only takes a few minutes to install. The first step is to go to Google's 2-Step Verification page, www.google.com/landing/2step, and click on the blue "Get Started" box in the upper right-hand corner. Enter your Gmail username and password and then click on the "Start Setup" button. Then, you will be asked to do something you won't want to do—enter your cell phone number. In order for 2FA to work and keep you safe, you're going to have to enter your cell phone number. (If you have Google Voice, don't use that number because you might get locked out.) Once Gmail has your cell phone number, you will receive a random six-digit number via a text message. A webpage will appear on the Gmail screen asking you to enter the six-digit code. You will then be asked whether or not to add your current computer as a trusted device and, if you're using a computer you normally use, you should answer *yes*. To install Google Authenticator, which I'd encourage you to do, download the app from Google Play and then go to the "2-step Verification" section of your Google account. Under "Set up alternative second step," find "Authenticator app" and tap "Set up." Follow the instructions on the screen, and get a code from your authenticator app to make sure it's working. These instructions work as of this writing, but, of course, Google might change their process at any time. The screens might not look identical when you try this for yourself.

Of course, there are millions of people around the world reading and writing email on their mobile devices, whether it's an iPhone, iPad, Android phone, or some other tablet. In fact, more than one-third of the people using email might be reading it on an iPhone or iPad, according to a 2018 survey by online marketing firm Litmus. They analyzed fifteen billion emails in the first half of 2018 and found that 29 percent were opened on iPhones, 10 percent on iPads, and 8 percent on Apple computers. About 27 percent were opened on Gmail and 7 percent on Outlook. Only 1 percent was opened on Yahoo! Mail, and I can't tell you how happy that makes me.

If you're using a device with an iOS platform to read and write email, I have good news: Apple also offers an easy process for installing two-factor authentication. With 2FA, your Apple ID and iCloud mail account can only be accessed on devices you trust, such as your iPhone, iPad, or Mac laptops and desktops. When you sign in to a new device for the first time, you'll have to enter your Apple ID password and a six-digit verification code that's automatically displayed on your trusted devices. By entering the code, you're verifying that you're currently working on a trusted device. Once you've signed in with a verification code, you won't be asked for it on that device again unless you sign out completely, erase the device, or change your Apple ID password for security reasons. You'll also be asked to enter a trusted telephone number to receive verification codes via text message or automated phone calls. To turn on two-factor authentication on your iPhone, iPad, or iPod touch (if you're using iOS 10.3 or later), go to Settings, sign in, and select "Password & Security." Tap the arrow next to "Turn On Two-Factor Authentication." Then tap "Continue" and a new screen will appear, where you'll be asked to enter a phone number to receive verification codes when you sign in. Enter a telephone number and tap "Next," and then a verification code will be sent to the phone number you provided. Enter the code to verify your phone number and turn on two-factor authentication. It's that easy. Like with Google, Apple might make a slight change at any time, so follow the most recent instructions.

Time for a quiz! Let's say you've just installed 2FA on your email account and you're sitting at the kitchen table. All of a sudden, your phone buzzes, notifying you that you've received a text message. You check the text message and see that it's a random six-digit code from Gmail. Since you're sitting at the table eating breakfast and reading email on your laptop, you know that you haven't logged on from an untrusted device. What happened? Someone else tried to log in to your Gmail account from an untrusted computer, probably after somehow stealing your username and password. But, since you'd taken the time to install 2FA, they still couldn't break into your account. How did they get that far? There might have been another data breach at a retailer, gas station, healthcare provider, or bank, which, unfortunately, seems to happen every day. Or maybe a keylogger was installed on your computer when your in-laws were using it. A bad guy took a swing and used the username and password from a different account across multiple platforms. What if your Gmail password was the same as your password for a bank website? Even though the would-be thief wasn't able to access your email, he might have still been able to use that same password to access your online banking. Hopefully, you've learned to protect yourself and not use the same passwords for every account, so you don't have anything to worry about.

Using separate passwords and 2FA is a great start. Now that you've locked down your email account, it's time to lock up your social media with 2FA.

HOW TO AVOID BECOMING A VICTIM

🔒 Realize that bad guys want to use your email account as a weapon to attack your family, friends, work colleagues, and others.

🔒 Only use email providers that offer two-factor authentication, such as Gmail, Outlook, and iCloud. You can find the providers that do and don't at www.twofactorauth.org.

🔒 Download an authenticator app like Duo Mobile, Google Authenticator, or Microsoft Authenticator on your smartphone from the Google Play Store or Apple App Store to randomly generate security codes rather than receiving them via text messages.

🔒 If you're using 2FA through SMS texting, create a list of ten backup 2FA codes for Google, and make them codes you'll remember but others won't recognize. Write them down and keep them in a safe place in case you lose your cell phone or can't receive the codes when using an untrusted device.

🔒 If you're using SMS, make sure you contact your cellular provider and implement a secret PIN code to ensure others can't access your number.

🔒 Don't access your email accounts from untrusted devices. Only access email from computers and mobile devices you own.

🔒 Avoid SMS-based 2FA for email accounts. There are more secure options out there, and SMS-based 2FA is vulnerable to SMS phishing and SIM hijacking, which are still somewhat effective.

CHAPTER 9

Social Media Safety

SOCIAL MEDIA DRIVES JUST ABOUT EVERYTHING IN TODAY'S
society, from fashion trends to politics to pop culture. It's absolutely
staggering how many people across the world are using apps like
Facebook, Twitter, Instagram, and LinkedIn. A recent survey by Sprout
Social Inc. found that 68 percent of U.S. adults between the ages of
eighteen to twenty-nine are using Facebook, which was expected to
generate $21.57 billion in U.S. advertising revenue in 2018. More than
one million hours of video is viewed on Facebook every single day!
Instagram has been growing rapidly, with about 60 percent of U.S.
adults on the Internet using it, and Twitter is most popular among
mobile users, with more than three hundred million users around the
world. Social media has literally changed the way we communicate and
document everything in our lives.

There's no question about it: Social media is an amazing tool that
can be used for both personal and professional purposes. However,
if social media is used without understanding the risks, it can destroy
a business, brand, or reputation. Am I saying you shouldn't use social
media? Absolutely not; I'm only saying you should use social media
wisely and use the built-in security features to keep yourself safe. Along
with playing nice on the net and refraining from bullying and other bad
behavior, we need to make sure we're protecting ourselves from the
bad guys lurking out there. If you still have doubts they're there, I have a
few Russian Facebook ads I'd like you to read. Believe me, social media
is a prime target for cybercriminals, and they can do a lot of irreparable
damage with surprisingly little effort.

Let me tell you about my friend Bill, who is the owner of a successful
real estate company and a heavy user of social media, both personally and professionally. Bill and I have been friends for a long time, and
I've given him a lot of tips about cybersecurity over the years. He still
uses my advice today to keep his company's information safe, which I
hope gives him a strategic advantage over his competitors. As a relo-
cation-company owner, Bill stores a lot of sensitive information for his
clients, and he knows how to keep it safe and secure. He uses social
media every day to stay in touch with his customers, and he routinely
provides them updates in the form of Facebook updates and tweets.

Of course, he employs my strategy of using separate passphrases for his mission-critical accounts and multifactor authentication on his social media platforms. He's way ahead of the game.

But nobody's perfect, and let's say, for example, that Bill's company Facebook account is compromised. It happens to companies around the world every day. What if Bill received a spear-phished email from either an *unknown* or a *known* sender (someone he knows and trusts), and then he clicked a link he should have stayed away from? Imagine, when Bill clicked the link, the bad guys installed a keylogger and stole his password. With Bill's username and password, the hackers could easily log in to his corporate Facebook account. Most organizations wouldn't be too concerned at this point, because their Facebook accounts certainly don't contain any sensitive information about their clients, such as date of birth, place of birth, bank accounts, credit cards, or Social Security numbers. But what if the hacker didn't even want that information? What if he was going after something much more important? What could possibly be more important? *Trust.* Corporate social media accounts are trusted platforms for clients, associates, and friends. And, if a bad guy is able to breach Bill's corporate platform, he can start pretending to be Bill.

Still with me? Good. Now let's assume the crook stole Bill's identity and became an imposter. He then has the ability to craft a message from Bill's Facebook account to all of his friends and clients, informing everyone that he has just landed a massive account that will take his company to new heights. Bill is so excited and grateful, the imposter tells them, and the only reason it happened was because of their over-whelming support and referrals. Bill wants to thank all of them by giving them a digital coupon for a free large cup of Starbucks coffee. Bill's friends and clients only have to click a link included in the message, and they'll be directed to a website where they can either print the coupon or store it electronically on their smartphones. Bill's friends and clients will probably believe the message is legitimate because he's successful and always generous. Now, the first time I ran this scenario by Bill, I asked him how many of his friends and clients would probably click the link and claim their free coffee. He guessed that 80–90 percent of them would probably do it.

You can guess the bad news. Imposter Bill wasn't interested in giving away free coffee. Instead, he probably set up a webserver on a compromised computer somewhere overseas. If Bill's friends and clients clicked the link, they would be taken to the bad guy's webserver, which would use a new strain of malware that isn't easily recognized by an intrusion detection system (IDS). As I told you earlier, malware writers are creating more than one hundred thousand new strains every day, and intrusion detection systems can't keep pace with the new strains until someone's computer is infected and it's reported. Let's say in Bill's case that most of his friends are employed and they're checking their Facebook accounts on company-owned computers like most U.S. workers do. When they click the link for the Starbucks coupon, they'll immediately infect their corporate network with a computer virus, which can cause their employer grave damage. The infiltration might include the installation of a keystroke logger, which steals multiple usernames and passwords for email and bank accounts. Or maybe it's ransomware, which will force their employer to pay tens of thousands of dollars to unlock the computers.

After going through each of these doomsday scenarios with Bill, I asked him, "How will your social media followers feel about you if you cause an outbreak of ransomware or malware at multiple corporations?" He guessed that no one would ever trust any email or social media message from him again, which would irreparably damage his company's brand. He finally admitted that he really needed to evaluate how his company used social media. I didn't advise him to stop using social media as a business tool; it can be very beneficial. He only needed to prevent cybercrooks from accessing his social media. How might he do that? With multifactor or two-factor authentication, which we discussed in the previous chapter.

Again, two-factor authentication is free and easy to set up. So, open Facebook's Security and Login page and find the options for two-factor authentication. You can choose to receive text messages on your cell phone or preferably an authentication app like Google Authenticator or

Duo Mobile. Facebook even allows you to receive alerts if anyone logs in to your account from an untrusted device, and you can choose three to five friends who can send you a code or URL from Facebook when you're locked out.

What if you don't use Facebook for business and only use to it share family photographs and recipes for your killer brisket? Is having two-factor authentication really that big of a deal? Well, the big deal happens when Boris Badenov takes over your Facebook account and crafts a really nice message from you, providing your family and friends with a funny kitten video with a message like, "Here is something to brighten your day." When two hundred of your closest friends and relatives receive the message and click the link, they'll be redirected to a computer overseas that will install a keystroke logger to steal usernames and passwords. You might not have many friends left afterward. That's the big deal!

At one point in my life, I swore I would never have a social media account; I just didn't think it was worth the risk. About eighteen months before I was eligible to retire from the Federal Bureau of Investigation, however, I took the plunge and got a LinkedIn account. I was heading up to the FBI office in Toronto for a thirty-day detail, and I wanted to connect with two old friends who were both on LinkedIn. Once I registered, I reconnected with a lot of old colleagues and made new connections through Cyber Subject Matter Experts. So much for never getting on social media! But I really believed LinkedIn was less dangerous because it was essentially a networking app for business professionals. Who would bother hacking that, right? I had new people asking to connect with me all the time, and LinkedIn seemed pretty harmless.

Each time someone wants to connect with you on LinkedIn, you receive an email from LinkedIn with a link. In reality, it's actually pretty easy for a bad guy to create a spoofed email from LinkedIn. What if the connection request was from someone you know? The email asks you to click a link to accept the person's request, or you can see a brief profile of the person making the request. I hope I would stick to my rule of thumb, *Think before you click.* I hope I wouldn't get caught up in the moment and accept the request from someone who I believed was an old friend or future business partner. To be sure, I've created an overriding rule or internal policy to reduce my risk: I will only accept requests from connections *within* LinkedIn. That means I delete the email, open my web browser, type www.linkedin.com to be sure I'm going to the *real* site, find the request in my in-app updates and notifications, and then accept the request from within the service. Or, I do this with the official LinkedIn app on my phone. This way, I avoid clicking any links in emails, thereby reducing my risk of malware infection. Honestly, you should use the same rule in all your social media platforms.

I now have close to three thousands contacts on my LinkedIn account. I was regularly sending out messages to my followers on how to stay safe on the Internet and how to avoid becoming a victim of cybercrime. I owe it my followers, and you owe it to each of your followers and friends, to keep your social media accounts safe. If a bad guy gained access to my account, he could easily send out a post that appeared to come from me, and then he could direct them to click a link to read a great article I recommended. I know most of my followers would click that link. But, instead of seeing something informative, the bad guy would take them to a website loaded with malicious code, where they'd become infected with malware. Infecting all of my followers would destroy my credibility as a cybersecurity expert—not to mention my sense of self-worth. So, what did I do? I installed 2FA. And I want you to do the same thing right now. Just click on Security Settings and follow the steps to implement two-factor authentication.

If you're avid Twitter user—and I'll admit that I'm not—it's painless to set up two-factor authentication there too. With the number of professional athletes, actresses, and politicians who are being exposed for the not-so-nice tweets of their youth, protecting your account might be essential in maintaining your reputation. You don't want a cybercriminal or a jilted lover taking over your account and tweeting photos or something obscene. Like Google and Facebook, you'll have to enter both your password and a code that's sent to your cell phone when you log in. The codes can be obtained via SMS texting or Google Authenticator, Duo Mobile, Authy, or a similar authentication app, which is much more secure.

One of my favorite things to do on LinkedIn is read articles that are recommended by my peers. What do I have to do to read them? I have to click a link in LinkedIn. How do I know these links are safe? Well, I don't. There's no sure way of knowing whether it's legitimate. But now that you know what can happen if you click on a link in an email, website, or social media, you hopefully know that it wouldn't be a good idea for a space shuttle pilot or nuclear power plant operator to check email, surf the web, or engage in social media on his work computer. But each one of us does it multiple times a day on multiple computers and mobile devices. This is one of the main reasons why cybercrime is out of control and will continue to get worse until we change the way we use computers.

HOW TO AVOID BECOMING A VICTIM

🔒 Install two-factor authentication on social media platforms such as Facebook, Twitter, Instagram, or LinkedIn.

🔒 If available, use authentication apps that don't rely on SMS texting for added security. If a social media app doesn't offer authentication through something other than text messages, I wouldn't use it until it does.

🔒 Only open links such as friend requests on Facebook and connection requests on LinkedIn through the actual apps or webpages. Don't click on the links that are sent through emails or messages to your phone.

🔒 Don't share too much information on social media. While most of us want everyone to know what we're doing, where we've been, and where we're going, sharing too much information makes you an easy target for identity theft. Never share your Social Security number, birth date, home address, or phone number on social media.

🔒 Don't post your work history on social media apps like Facebook. By advertising where you worked and when you were there, you're providing cybercriminals with a lot of the information they'll need to fill out fraudulent loan applications in your name.

🔒 Customize the privacy settings on social media apps. Take control of who can see what you're posting and limit what personal information is shared with others.

🔒 We love to post photographs from our family vacations, but it's also an advertisement to criminals that it's a good time to break into our homes. And, if we've posted too much information on social media, the bad guys probably know exactly where we live.

CHAPTER 10

Is the Cloud Safe?

ONE OF THE QUESTIONS I GET ASKED MOST OFTEN IS, "IS THE cloud safe?" Some people I talk to even ask, "What is the cloud?" And, no, I'm not talking about the big, white, fluffy things up in the sky. There are a lot of different names for the types of clouds I'm talking about: public cloud, private cloud, Software as a Service (SaaS), Infrastructure as a Service (IaaS), file hosting service, and even hybrid cloud. My definition of the cloud is a little simpler. I define it as *a computer that doesn't belong to you, but it's where you store your information.* Think of it as a hopefully secure space you're leasing, or, in many cases, it's where you're storing your stuff for free. If you use Google, iCloud, Outlook, Dropbox, Microsoft, or Quickbooks, you're using a cloud. We store files, documents, music, and photos in the cloud so we can keep it safe and access it from anywhere in the world. Because of the cloud, we no longer have to store our information on the hard drive of a device or carry it around on a tiny thumb drive that we almost always lose. For a lot of reasons, the cloud is a really great invention.

The cloud is an especially important and amazing tool for small businesses. It can be used to store files and share files between clients and colleagues when they might otherwise be too large to send through emails. Most cloud-based services store three copies of documents that are uploaded, so there's no danger of losing important work. Most options are cost-effective compared to other types of web-hosting services, and you're not required to purchase new hardware every time you need more storage space. Plus, you don't have worry about a server going down, which might affect an employee's productivity and ability to access important documents.

But, much like everything else on the Internet, the cloud has the potential of being extremely dangerous. One weekend about ten years ago, I went scanner crazy. I decided it was finally time for the Augenbaum family to go green and paperless, so I took all our important documents out of a fireproof lock box and started scanning them. Since I'd already spent my hard-earned money on a digital scanner, I figured I might as well use it. What a great idea! I scanned all our birth certificates, passports, Social Security cards, marriage certificate, and state and federal tax returns. Then, I saved all the documents to a folder called

"Important Documents" on my computer's internal hard drive. This was *not* a smart idea. I might as well have labeled it, "Bad Guys: This Is What You're Looking For!" To make matters worse, the file wasn't even password-protected. I figured that, since I'd gone through the trouble of backing up my important documents on my hard drive, I might as well have a backup of the backup. Now, the smart thing would have been to burn the file to a CD or save it on a thumb drive or external hard drive that I could keep in a secure location at home or safe deposit box at a bank. But, no, I saved the file to my Google Drive cloud account! For weeks, I'd been receiving a bunch of emails from Google, informing me that I had a gigabyte of free storage space on my Google Drive account. So, I uploaded all of my important documents there.

Hopefully, a few things should be jumping out to you by now. If I only need a username and password to access my account from anywhere in the world, who else could access my sensitive information? Well, if a bad guy steals my username and password, he could easily break in. This brings me back to my earlier question: *is the cloud safe?* Despite the scenario I just described to you, the answer is *yes*. The bad guys don't typically hack into an actual cloud provider; they don't need to. The files you send to the cloud are being stored on hard drives on machines that are heavily secured in data centers around the country. It would be pretty difficult for a cybercrook to penetrate them. Instead, it's a lot easier to attack the end users—you and me. The only things a bad guy needs to break into a cloud account are the username and password, and then it's usually game over for the victim. But, since you're now an expert in creating passphrases and installing two-factor authentication, hopefully you understand the importance of keeping your cloud accounts safe and realize how easy it is to lock them down.

Along with Google Drive, another cloud provider that is chock-full of sensitive information is Dropbox, a file hosting service that offers cloud storage, file synchronization, personal cloud, and client software for free. I've seen a lot of corporations use it to store sensitive work projects so their employees can access the files from work and home. In February 2018, Dropbox announced that it had more than five hundred million users who had uploaded more than four hundred *billion* pieces of content. About 1.2 billion files are being uploaded to Dropbox every single day! Many people use the Dropbox app on their cell phones to download and access files; the app has been downloaded onto Android phones more than five hundred million times.

One night, while I was writing this book, I went upstairs and found a nice, quiet place to hide and write. Much to my surprise, I found my wife's laptop opened to her Dropbox account. As a trained cyber-investigator and nosey person in general, I noticed that her Dropbox account contained about 715 MB of accounting and tax documents belonging to her clients. To my horror (but not my surprise), I discovered that two-factor authentication hadn't been turned on. I went to "Settings" and clicked on "Security," and, at the bottom of the screen, was "Two-Step Verification"—which had been turned off. I enabled and provided her cell phone number to receive the code. Then, her account and all her clients' personal information were secure. Unsecured Dropbox accounts present an enormous opportunity for cybercriminals, and I guarantee you that they're constantly scheming for ways to break in.

Many workers in corporate America use Dropbox as an easy way to move and share large files. Do you think it's a good idea for your doctor to use Dropbox to access your medical records from his home computer or anywhere else in the world? Some might say it's a great idea, because he could save lives and work more efficiently. But what if your doctor has a Yahoo! account that was hacked by criminals who stole his username and password—the same login credentials he also used for Dropbox? Unfortunately, we know the end result: Bad guys could gain access to sensitive personal files, including your medical records. Am I saying you shouldn't use Dropbox? No; I'm saying it's a great tool and you *should* use it—but only if you're using two-factor authentication to secure your information.

Google Drive and Dropbox aren't the only clouds being used to store accounting, medical, and payroll records. I had one case while I was working for the FBI that involved crooks gaining access to an accountant's cloud-based software package. His email was hacked and, unfortunately, he used the same password for his cloud-based software. The bad guys were able to access his clients' names, dates of birth, Social Security numbers, email addresses, and bank account and routing numbers. He had to pay an expensive security firm to come in and clean up the mess. He also had to notify his customers that he'd lost their information, which I'm sure cost him some business. This victim admitted to me that the incident cost him more than $75,000 after all was said and done. A Big Four accounting firm can handle a financial loss like that, but it took a lot of hard work to keep this small business from going under.

In another case, cybercriminals gained access to a small business' payroll platform by logging in with stolen usernames and passwords. With the stolen information, the thieves changed bank account and routing numbers to bank accounts they controlled. The bad guys walked away with more than $100,000, and the company was forced out of business.

Unfortunately, cybercriminals like to target small businesses because they don't have the high-priced cybersecurity they need. A Verizon study found that 61 percent of cyberattack victims in 2017 were small businesses, up from 53 percent the previous year. Another report by Hiscox found that 47 percent of small businesses suffered at least one cyberattack in the previous twelve months and 52 percent suffered multiple attacks. Like it wasn't hard enough to keep a small business open nowadays!

The biggest target for cloud attacks is Microsoft Office 365. In the old days, you purchased a hard copy of Microsoft Office, loaded the software to your computer, and went to work. Then, in June 2011, Microsoft introduced Office 365, giving consumers the ability to download Office software and store information in the cloud. It was cheaper and more efficient, but now the bad guys only needed usernames and passwords to attack. They didn't have to break into an office computer or network, which formerly stored the sensitive information. In 2017, there was a sophisticated cloud-to-cloud brute-force attack against Office 365 users who worked at multiple Fortune 2,000 companies. The attackers tried logging in with different versions of Office 365 usernames, which suggested they'd *already* obtained some version of them through another breach or phishing attack. In a separate 2018 phishing attack, cybercriminals attempted to dupe users and steal millions of Office 365 passwords by disguising malicious emails as tax-related notifications from the Internal Revenue Service.

Microsoft recently asked YouGov, the Internet market research firm, to conduct a survey of one thousand small business owners on its behalf. Shockingly, about 71 percent of small business owners who were surveyed said they believe they are at risk of falling victim to a cyberattack. Not surprisingly, only 50 percent of them were using some form of email encryption, and about 59 percent had no way of remotely wiping data from a lost or stolen device. Even worse, more than half of them said they handled Social Security numbers and 29 percent stored bank records. In most of the Office 365 breaches of the past, the bad guys gained access because users who were logging in remotely hadn't installed two-factor authentication. Once their usernames and passwords were stolen, the crooks had access to everything in the company. The breaches weren't necessarily Microsoft's fault, though; it was the Office 365 users—people like us—who had dropped the ball by not keeping their information secure.

When I speak at business conferences, I always make it clear that it doesn't matter how much money you spend on information security products if you don't use two-factor authentication for remote employees. I usually raise my voice when I'm talking about this subject, but I'm tired of dealing with issues that could have been easily avoided. Most of the people I talk to at technology conferences tell me there have been very few breaches in the cloud, and most that *have* occurred were actually computers breaches within the victim organization itself—not at the cloud-server provider. I always reply that bad guys are targeting end users and not cloud providers, and then I try to explain what steps they should take to keep their clients safe. I tell them they need to make sure to have separate passwords, a strong, robust password for their cloud account, and to only use cloud providers that offer 2FA.

If you search online, there are thousands of cloud providers, and every one of them wants your business. Each provider lists numerous ways they can take your business to the next level without having to spend a pile of cash. When searching for a cloud-based solution for either home or work, you need to make sure the provider offers two-factor authentication. Most cloud providers now offer the option, but, unfortunately, most users don't end up using it. Go to https://twofactorauth.org/#cloud to find out which cloud providers have two-factor authorization. And, as I said about email and social media in previous chapters, if your cloud provider doesn't offer 2FA, you need to find one that does. It's that simple.

Before you decide to use a cloud service, there are a couple of questions you need to ask yourself. What exactly are you storing in the cloud? Is it sensitive personal information? Do you really need to keep copies of your passport, driver's license, birth certificate, and bank records in Google Drive or Microsoft's OneDrive? What do you need to store in the cloud if you own a small business? Should you really store your clients' personal and financial information and employees' personal and payroll information there?

If you want to store everything in the cloud, you'd better make darn sure that you're using two-factor authentication and that you have a good plan in place in case a bad guy gains access to your cloud account. Is there a real person you can call to resolve the situation quickly? Are there difficult challenge questions in place to keep the bad guys out? Those are the important questions you must ask yourself before deciding to use a cloud-based service. Your company's well-being and your family's future might depend on it.

HOW TO AVOID BECOMING A VICTIM

🔒 Decide if you really need cloud-based storage. Would you be better off keeping the information you're storing in a safe or safe deposit box?

🔒 If you decide to use a cloud, only choose a provider that offers two-factor authentication and make sure you turn it on. You can identify clouds that offer 2FA at https://twofactorauth.org/#cloud.

🔒 Be sure to use a different password for your cloud accounts. Passwords should be at least twelve characters long (fifteen is even better) and include lower- and uppercase letters, numbers, and at least one special character.

🔒 If you're a small-business owner, educate your employees about their responsibility in securing their usernames and passwords. Set up emergency protocols in response to potential breaches.

🔒 Make sure you have backups of whatever you store in the cloud, whether it's on external hard drives or other offsite storage.

🔒 Use cloud encryption, which is critical for protection. It allows data and text to be transformed using encryption algorithms and then placed on a storage cloud.

CHAPTER 11

Business Email Compromise

ONE OF THE LARGEST CYBERCRIME THREATS IN THE WORLD IS
called the business email compromise scheme (BEC), also known as
cyber-enabled financial fraud. This attack is carried out by compromising
legitimate personal and business email accounts through old-fashioned
social engineering, computer intrusion techniques, and stealing usernames and passwords. BEC criminals *trick* end users into either wiring
them money or sending them names, dates of birth, and Social Security
numbers. According to the FBI's Internet Crime Complaint Center (IC3),
the BEC scam continues to grow, evolve, and target end users of all
varieties. Since the FBI started formally keeping track of BEC and its
variant, email account compromise (EAC), there have been reported
losses of $12 billion through June 2018. Foreign citizens perpetrated
many of the schemes, which originated in Nigeria but have since spread
across the globe. Reports indicate that fraudulent transfers have been
sent to one hundred and fifteen countries, with the majority going
to Asian banks located in China and Hong Kong. During my career, I
found instances in which money was transferred to dozens of foreign
countries.

In June 2018, the FBI and Department of Justice announced a major
coordinated law enforcement effort to disrupt BEC schemes that
were designed to intercept and hijack wire transfers from businesses
and individuals. Operation WireWire, which also included agents from
the Department of Homeland Security, Department of Treasury, and
the U.S. Postal Inspection Service, resulted in seventy-four arrests,
including forty-two people in the U.S., twenty-nine in Nigeria, and three
in Canada, Mauritius, and Poland. The six-month operation resulted
in the seizure of nearly $2.4 million and the disruption and recovery
of almost $14 million in fraudulent wire transfers. Occasionally, even
though it is extremely difficult, we are actually able to locate, arrest,
and punish the bad guys.

I investigated hundreds of BEC cases while working for the FBI,
and I saw everyone from homeowners, small businesses, healthcare
companies, real estate firms, and even large corporations targeted in
these scams. The worst part is that every one of these crimes could
have been avoided. One of the cases I worked involved a small nonprofit

organization that had a wonderful mission of funding projects to help feed children in impoverished countries. Elena worked as the finance manager for the nonprofit, and one day her boss, Jeremy, was out of the office soliciting donations. Of course, fundraising is the lifeblood of any nonprofit, and it was Elena's job to keep track of the money that was coming in and going out. On this day, Elena received an email from Jeremy instructing her to wire $35,000 to a bank account in West Africa as part of a humanitarian effort. This request wasn't particularly unusual, so Elena followed Jeremy's instructions. She called the bank and directed someone there to wire the money to the account in West Africa. During their conversation, the bank representative warned Elena of something called a business email compromise and questioned whether a cybercriminal might be impersonating her boss. Elena assured the banker that it was a legitimate transaction and there was nothing to worry about.

The following week at a management meeting, Elena provided an update of the money that had been raised and where it had been sent for humanitarian projects. When Elena mentioned the $35,000 wire transfer to West Africa, Jeremy interrupted her with a puzzled look.

"*Where* did you send $35,000?" Jeremy asked. "And *why* did you send it there?"

Elena was surprised by Jeremy's concerned tone and wondered if he had simply forgotten. She explained that she'd received his email, which included instructions for wiring the money to a bank account in West Africa. When Jeremy claimed he'd never sent Elena such an email, she pulled out her laptop and showed him the email. Jeremy opened his outbox, which didn't contain the email in question. Upon further examination of the header pulled off the email in question, it became clear what had happened. Jeremy's email address was Jeremy@nonprofit.com (used only for example); the email Elena received was from Jeremy@nonprofit.com. It might take you a second to notice the difference, but that's exactly what cybercriminals want to happen. It's such a subtle disparity that most people would probably never recognize it. In most instances, we don't pay close attention to the addresses on the emails we receive—especially if they're from someone we know. Jeremy was obviously upset and confused, so he took his anger out on Elena. Jeremy called the bank and demanded it take action, but the only thing the bank could do was attempt to recall the wire transfer. Sadly, your chances of recalling an international wire transfer after twenty-four hours are slim to none. Then the banker explained to Jeremy that he'd warned Elena about BEC scams when she called to request the wire transfer. Things weren't getting better for her.

While investigating this case, I discovered the nonprofit organization was not utilizing two-factor authentication, and the bad guy had gained access to Jeremy's email account—probably through password reuse or a keystroke logger. The thief read Jeremy's emails and figured out how the organization conducted business, and he quickly realized that he only needed to send Elena an email with wire transfer instructions to steal the nonprofit's money. The cybercriminal then registered a looka-like domain (the company name after the @ symbol in an email address) to mimic the nonprofit's actual domain. When Elena received the email from Jeremy, she reasonably assumed it was from him and had the bank wire the money.

During the course of our investigation, we discovered the crook was using a free web hosting service. We served the web hosting company with a federal grand jury subpoena, but the only breadcrumb of a clue was the IP address, which is almost always registered in West Africa. The bad guys are smart enough not to provide their actual names and addresses when they register phony websites. In the old days, the easiest way to catch a crook was to follow the money. Today, the bad guys send stolen money to overseas banks accounts, and it's nearly impossible to find them and recover the funds. It's an enormous red flag for most companies to receive a request to send money overseas, so the cybercriminals recruit *mules* in the U.S. to do their dirty work. Mules are witting or unwitting accomplices who facilitate transfers to over-seas banks or, in some cases, receive stolen money into their domestic accounts and then wire the money to the thief from there. Mules who *knowingly* participate in the scam receive a small fraction of the stolen money for their trouble.

The largest victim of a BEC scheme that I ever worked with was a small company that lost $7.5 million. The company's chief executive officer was traveling overseas, and a bad guy spoofed an email to the finance manager that was allegedly from the CEO. In the email, the impostor claimed he'd been forced to set up a new email account because he was out of the country and couldn't trust the network security in his hotel. The impostor told the finance manager that he was working on a highly sensitive business transaction, and he directed the manager to await instructions from an attorney who would tell him how to proceed. A few hours later, the finance manager received an email from the attorney and then followed instructions to wire transfer $7.5 million to a bank in Hong Kong. To make matters worse, the CEO and finance manager didn't talk for the next two weeks. By the time the CEO returned to the U.S. and discovered that his company had been victimized, it was too late to take action. I've seen numerous cases in which money was sent to banks in Hong Kong and China, where banking and privacy laws make it nearly impossible to obtain information, even for law enforcement. Their laws allow cybercriminals to act with impunity.

Why was it so easy for cybercriminals to pull off a $7.5 million heist? Unfortunately, we tend to trust what's included in our emails, and we rarely verify their contents by calling the sender on the phone. Cybercrooks have been able to swindle $12 billion through BEC schemes. This not only harms victims but also severely damages the global economy. There's a pretty simple solution: *we must stop assuming every email can be trusted.* I've had vendors approach me about products that are allegedly like silver bullets that supposedly reduce risk by keeping emails secure. However, I don't think you should take a bad business process, wrap it in technology, and hope for the best. Instead, let's create a policy that prohibits money from being transferred based on what someone's read in an email or text message. Let's require anyone wiring money to bank accounts in the U.S. or overseas to receive verification—either over the phone or in person. While it might seem like common sense for many people, that simple business practice would have prevented several of the problems I've discussed.

I hate to say it, but that change might not be enough to eliminate BEC scams. The bad guys are constantly identifying weak business practices and inventing devious ways to exploit them. I'll give you a good example: In my years at the FBI, I'd receive a flurry of calls from panicked CEOs or in-house accountants prior to April 15, which is the annual federal tax deadline for U.S. citizens. It happened every year because the crooks had undoubtedly devised a new way to exploit office managers, human resource officers, accountants, and anyone else working in payroll and taxes. In one case I investigated, a cybercriminal targeted a human resources department with a spoofed email that was supposedly sent from a company executive. The impostor requested every employee's personally identifiable information and W-2 form for tax and audit purposes. In one week, I received phone calls from people at seven different companies that were victimized by this specific BEC scam. In each instance, the victims sent their employees' sensitive information to the cybercriminals, and they couldn't understand why they were targeted since they didn't maintain employee information on their company websites. They were amazed when I showed them how the bad guys were able to target their workers through LinkedIn and other social media. Is this common practice in most businesses? What would the new HR officer in your company do if he or she received an email from the boss asking for this information? It only takes a phone call or face-to-face meeting to prevent something bad from happening.

One of the most frustrating aspects of investigating cybercrime for the FBI was that, as soon as we educated the public on one type of BEC scam, the bad guys came up with another variation. It was almost impossible to keep up! In another case I investigated, Company X purchased an expensive widget from Company Y for $3.5 million. Once the transaction was approved, someone from Company Y emailed an invoice for $3.5 million to the accounts payable department at Company X. This type of transaction occurs in corporate America thousands of times every day. Company X's accounts payable department was aware the invoice was coming, so the clerk started the process of arranging the payment. About an hour later, however, the clerk received another email from Company Y, which informed her that the initial invoice was incorrect and the company had been mistakenly overcharged $3,000. A second invoice containing the correct amount was being sent right away. So, what did the accounts payable clerk do? You guessed it. She started the process of paying the lesser total; five levels of management had to sign off on such a large invoice. Each person in the chain of command approved the payment, and, after the company's top manager signed off, she initiated a wire transfer from Company X to Company Y for $3.497 million.

About ten days later, an accountant from Company Y sent an email to the accountants payable clerk at Company X with a friendly reminder about the outstanding $3.5 million balance. Obviously, the email caused quite a stir at Company X. The employees there checked the original email to see where the money was sent, and they discovered it was wired to Company Y's bank account in the Middle East. There was only one problem: Company Y didn't have a bank account in the Middle East! By the time someone from Company X called me to help, it was too late. The bad guys had already withdrawn the money from the bank account they controlled. And, due to the country's bank privacy laws, the bank wouldn't share information without a mutual legal assistance treaty that required me to get approval from the U.S. Department of Justice—something that would have taken months. My FBI colleague in this country told me he saw this type of illegal activity every day.

Company X had a $10 million cyber-liability insurance policy; unfortunately, it was told this type of fraud wasn't covered. The fraud policy only covered a loss if there were *two parties* involved in the authentication of a wire transfer. However, the accounts payable clerk at Company X never contacted anyone at Company Y before the money was sent. If she had reached out to someone there to verify the account number and new invoice total, she probably would have been told it was indeed legitimate—because she would have called the phone number on the bogus second email that the bad guys had sent. It would have been a lookalike domain that *appeared* to be from Company Y. Even though she probably still would have sent the money, the act of trying to verify the wire transfer details would have been enough to activate their insurance policy. Too late.

Company X ended up spending $50,000 on private investigators who tried to track the criminals down. Guess what the investigators discovered? The cyberthieves had taken over a high-ranking employee's email account at Company X because the company didn't use two-factor authentication. The bad guys read his emails and discovered that Company Y was getting ready to send an invoice for $3.5 million. They set up a forwarding rule in the company's email system and, when Company Y sent the invoice to Company X, they intercepted the email and sent the fraudulent invoice.

As a result of this very expensive lesson, the accounts payable clerk was fired (because someone always gets fired in cases like these). But was the right person terminated? Did Company X have a policy in place that required voice confirmation whenever a bank account number is changed? The clerk was only doing her job. If the company had used two-factor authentication, the bad guys would have never cracked into the high-ranking employee's email to know the transaction was about to take place. Furthermore, one of my sources at the company told me the information security manager proposed requiring two-factor authentication about a year before the incident. Upper management rejected his recommendation because it didn't want to spend the money and time on something that was such "a pain in the rear" to use.

So, I'll ask the question again: Was the right person fired?

HOW TO AVOID BECOMING A VICTIM

🔒 Implement two-factor authentication for any wire transfer.

🔒 Never send a wire transfer based on the contents of an email; call someone directly or meet face-to-face with the person initiating or invoicing the wire transfer to verify the payment details.

🔒 Utilize two-factor authentication for company email. Most BEC scams are successful because cybercriminals gain access to employees' email accounts.

🔒 Before wiring the money, verify the bank account and routing numbers with account numbers you have on hand. If it's the first transaction with a new vendor, call someone at the company to verify the bank information.

🔒 If you're calling someone at a new vendor to verify bank information, call a phone number you have on hand or search for the number in a directory. Don't call the number included in the email.

🔒 Compare the email address on invoices with email addresses you've previously received from the company. Verify that the invoice wasn't sent from a spoofed email account.

🔒 When replying to a suspicious or mission-critical email, use your email program's *Forward* button instead of *Reply*. Then, type in the known email address of the person who allegedly sent you the message. By forwarding instead of replying to the message, you protect yourself from replying back to an illegitimate email from a spoofed account.

🔒 Register any company domains that might be slightly different than your *actual* company domain. For instance, if your company's domain is jerrysbagels.com, then register jerrysbagels.co, jerrybagels.com, and jerrysbagles.com. This will help prevent cybercriminals from registering spoofed domains.

🔒 Establish one-time passwords or security questions for employees who might be traveling and might not have access to their phones. If an employee requests a wire transfer from the road, require that he or she provide the password or answers. Make sure the passwords and questions are strong.

🔒 If you receive emails containing the phrases "code to admin expenses" or "urgent wire transfer," be extra diligent about verifying their legitimacy. Victims of previous BEC scams reported those phrases were included in spoofed emails.

CHAPTER 12

Real Estate Rip-Offs

THOUSANDS OF HOMES ARE SOLD EVERY DAY ACROSS THE country. People who have worked hard and saved for years to purchase their dream homes are boxing up their belongings, preparing to put down new roots, and getting ready to make what will probably be the biggest financial transaction of their lives. Unfortunately, it only takes a cybercriminal a few minutes to spoil the American dream for a hopeful homebuyer.

One of the most rapidly growing and financially damaging business email compromise scams targets people working in the real estate industry: buyers, sellers, real estate agents, mortgage brokers, bankers, and title insurance companies. Problems begin to arise when a cybercriminal compromises an email account of someone involved in the transaction—such as the buyer, seller, real estate agent, or closing attorney—and then creates a domain that is nearly identical. He'll send an email to the buyers or someone at the title company, providing them with new bank account information for a down payment, closing costs, or the final purchase price. In many of these cases, the stolen money isn't wired overseas, because that request would cause a big red flag for the would-be homebuyer. Instead, the bad guys will use a mule account to acquire the stolen funds before sending it overseas.

In July 2018, the FBI's Internet Complaint Center (IC3) reported that cybercriminals were increasingly stealing funds from the real estate sector, including title companies, law firms, real estate agents, buyers, and sellers. IC3 reported that fraud reports from people who were victimized by BEC scams involving real estate transactions increased by 1,100 percent from 2015 to 2017. And, in the same time frame, the money lost to such scams increased by 2,200 percent, peaking at more than $18 million during the quarter ending in October 2017. In 2017 alone, IC3 reported receiving more than nine thousand complaints of online real estate fraud that resulted in losses of more than $56 million. In only the past few years, I've seen dozens of victims in Nashville, Tennessee, with losses totaling millions of dollars.

Businesses of all sizes have fallen victim to this BEC scam, and the cyberthieves are even tricking some very smart people. In June 2017, New York State Supreme Court Justice Lori Sattler was scammed out of more than $1 million after she was duped while trying to sell her apartment and buy another one. According to published reports, Sattler was attempting to purchase a new apartment when she received an email that she believed was sent by her real estate attorney. The person claiming to be Sattler's lawyer instructed her to wire $1.057 million to a specific bank account. Her stolen money was then forwarded to Commerce Bank of China, according to the reports. In August 2017, a Washington, D.C., couple was scammed out of $1.5 million as they prepared to purchase their dream home. The couple, both of whom were federal government workers, planned to use an inheritance to purchase a bigger home for their family. They put down a $200,000 down payment and were preparing for closing when they received an email that appeared to come from their title company. They replied to the email, which instructed them to wire the remaining $1.5 million to a bank account. But, when the couple arrived at the attorney's office on the day of the closing, they were informed they'd been scammed. Investigators discovered that a cybercriminal had hacked into someone's email account at the title company and spoofed an email to the couple. The victims notified the FBI and sued the title company in hopes of recovering their stolen money. They were still able to purchase the home with the rest of their inheritance, the published reports said, but they never saw that $1.5 million again.

After the first traumatic experience, victims of real estate BEC scams usually don't fall for them again—but it should never have happened in the first place. When an email account is compromised, the bad guys read all the emails and it doesn't take them long to figure out how a business operates. In one of the cases I investigated, the victim was a title insurance company. Title insurance protects buyers and mortgage lenders against defects or fraud with a title when a property is sold or transferred; a title company researches records to ensure that there are no undisclosed heirs to the property, unpaid taxes, pending legal action, errors, or fraud associated with the title. This particular company outsourced most of its information technology infrastructure to a capable IT provider, which clearly understood information security. They had an excellent firewall established for the company and also installed an effective enter-prise-level information security suite. The title company was better protected than most small companies.

Unfortunately, the bad guys were able to obtain the username and password for a real estate agent, whom we'll call Amanda. She was representing clients who were in the process of selling a home. Amanda had a Gmail account with an email address of Amanda1935@gmail.com (only an example) and did not have two-factor authentication turned on. How did the bad guys gain access to her Gmail account? She might have clicked on a link she shouldn't have clicked on, which would have allowed the cybercriminals' malware to install a keylogger on her computer and steal her password. Or maybe there was an unreported data breach at a large supermarket, gas station, department store, or pharmacy, and Amanda's username and password were among the ones stolen. Then the bad guys probably could have counted on Amanda being among the 60—70 percent of the U.S. population that uses the same password for every online platform. This scenario prob-ably sounds familiar to you by now, because it's the genesis for almost every cybercrime. Armed with Amanda's username and password, the cybercriminals could have easily logged into her Gmail account. If she had only installed two-factor authentication on her Gmail, the crooks wouldn't have been able to break into it.

While reading Amanda's emails, the bad guys discovered that she represented a couple that was getting ready to close a real estate trans-action, and that Amanda was communicating with a woman we'll call Beverly at a title company. The cybercriminals learned the closing date was only a couple of days away. So, the bad guys registered an email account at a free email provider in the name of Amanda1935@mail.com, and they were ready for business. They broke back into Amanda's Gmail account and set up a simple forwarding rule. Any email that the title company sent to Amanda's Gmail account would be forwarded to them. Then the criminals sent an email to Beverly from their spoof email account. The subject line said, "Change of Plans," and the message read, "Hi, Beverly, hope all is well. My clients just called and they want the proceeds of the sale to be wired to a different bank account. I hope this isn't too much of a pain in the butt. Please tell me what I need to do. Have a blessed day." Since the bad guys had access to Amanda's emails, they were able to write the email as if it came from her, using the same language, structure, and closing phrase.

Beverly quickly responded to the email, "This happens all the time, Amanda. Just send me the new bank account information." Once Beverly received an email from the fake Amanda1935@mail.com address with the new bank information, she replaced the sellers' account with the one controlled by the cybercriminals.

The closing went off without a hitch at the attorney's office, but then, a few days later, the sellers complained that they still had not received $250,000 from the sale. The title company discovered that the money had been sent to a bank in Texas, and that's when the finger-pointing started. By the time I was called in to help about ten days later, the money was long gone. I contacted the bank and my contact there provided me with the account history and a fake West African passport, which the thief had used to open the account. He'd even gone to the Texas Secretary of State's website and registered a business in one of the seller's name, and the state provided him with a legitimate tax ID number. Then the bad guy, armed with the fake passport and real tax ID number, went to the bank and opened an account. As soon as the stolen money was wired to the account, he cashed it out in ten cashier's checks ranging from $18,000 to $25,000. Each of the cashier's checks was written to someone different; the names matched the ones on the criminal's fake passports. Once those checks were cashed, most of the money was sent to Nigeria. Our law enforcement partners were essentially chasing ghosts, and the money was already overseas.

The title company discovered it was legally obligated to pay the sellers their stolen money. It could have gone after Amanda, but she was only a part-time agent and didn't have much money. She lost her commission on the sale, though, and her reputation as a dependable real estate agent was damaged forever. Beverly was fired for her mistake, even though she was only following the procedures that were in place at her employer. Someone *always* gets fired in these cases, remember?

Going back to the important points I made earlier:

1. Once your money is stolen, it is hard to recover.
2. The FBI's chances of identifying the cybercriminals and putting them in jail are surprisingly low.
3. This type of crime could be prevented about 90 percent of the time.

How could this crime have been stopped? If Amanda had installed two-factor authentication on her Google account, the interlopers would have never gained access to it. But Amanda shouldn't get all the blame, either. If the title company had implemented one simple policy, the entire mess might have been avoided. It should have had this rule in place: *any changes to the distribution of proceeds from sale must be accompanied by a follow-up telephone call for verification.* But even that policy could probably use a little more tweaking. What if Beverly had sent an email to Amanda1935@mail.com and said, "You know the policy; you need to call me." Then the bad guys might have called pretending to be Amanda with a cold, or they could have sent an email saying, "I can't get to the phone, but my assistant will call you in a few minutes." Or, even better, Beverly could have forwarded the "Change of Plans" email to Amanda at the address she knew to be correct instead of replying to the new mission-critical (and spoofed) message. It's up to the title company to develop an airtight policy to prevent millions of dollars from being stolen. If it doesn't make necessary changes, it might continue to be victimized.

It's so important that proper policies are in place and that they are shared with all third parties. A five-alarm siren needs to sound anytime someone wants to change bank account information. Everyone in the company needs to be suspicious of such changes and follow up with foolproof verification that *doesn't* involve email or text. There was a time when people had to appear in person at real estate closings, but technology has spoiled us and we're too accustomed to a streamlined business process. But it's our insistence on being fast and efficient that has gotten us into all of this trouble. The criminals are winning. They've stolen billions and billions of dollars—and that's only what's been reported.

I have drafted a simple and realistic policy for real estate trans-actions, which is this: A title company must tell all its employees that any changes to bank information must be verified, but not by email or text. The title company employees must pass this information to real estate agents, closing attorneys, buyers, and sellers. That way, there won't be any surprises. Executives need to explain to every one of their employees that, if they fall victim to a BEC scam, they're going to be fired. That might sound harsh, but these victims don't *have* to be victims. A little caution and common sense will correct some of these prob-lems. If a client is located out of town, you better know what he or she looks like and then have a videoconference to verify any changes to the closing process. Will this slow things down? Of course, but it's better to be safe than sorry, especially when it comes to potentially losing millions of dollars.

When I was still working for the FBI, I shared this policy sugges-tion during one of my presentations to real estate executives. A woman in the audience complained that it would be too difficult to implement. I understood and joked that nobody wants a guy from the federal government telling the private sector how to do its job. But it's all about prevention, and if someone calls the FBI after the crime has already been committed, there's sadly little it can do.

Unfortunately, many real estate agents are using unsecured AOL and Yahoo! accounts to do business, and they're using these accounts to communicate with homebuyers and sellers every day. The bad guys will continue to target the real estate sector as long as these companies continue to do business as usual. But what about you? What are you going to do the next time you buy or sell a house and a title company or real estate broker sends you an email instructing you to send 20 percent of your down payment to a certain bank account and routing number? If you've read this far, you're hopefully going to pick up the phone and verify or, better yet, go to the office in person.

HOW TO AVOID BECOMING A VICTIM

🔒 Raise awareness in your company about the threat of business email compromise scams, which will make your company less likely to become a victim.

🔒 Do not accept any changes to bank account information via email or text messages. Require employees to verify each bank change, preferably in person or at least over the phone.

🔒 Ask your bank to hold customer requests for international wire transfers for an additional period of time to verify the legitimacy of the requests.

🔒 Be especially suspicious of requests for secrecy or pressure to take action quickly.

🔒 Don't call the phone number that's included in the email requesting the bank change. Call a previously known number that's listed in a directory or included on a business card.

🔒 Carefully scrutinize all emails related to real estate transactions, paying special attention to the sender's email address. Make certain it's not a spoofed email account and compare it to other emails you've received from that person in the past.

🔒 If your real estate agent prefers to use a personal email account to conduct business, ask that she or he only communicate with you through company email. It's probably more secure.

🔒 If you're a buyer or seller, never rely on information about a wire transfer that's included in emails or text messages. Call your real estate agent, closing attorney, or someone at the title company and inform them that you've received an email or text message and want to verify its contents.

🔒 Install two-factor authentication on your email. Ask your real estate agent, closing attorney, and representative of the title company if they're utilizing 2FA, as well.

CHAPTER 13

Work-from-Home Nightmares

THERE'S A LOT TO LOVE ABOUT WORKING FROM HOME: NOT
sitting behind a desk from nine to five, avoiding traffic or crowded
subways and buses, saving a few bucks on lunch and your professional wardrobe, and having the flexibility to spend more time with your
family and friends during the work week. More and more Americans
are working remotely, and it's pretty easy to see why it's so enticing for
employees and their employers, who have figured out that their workers
are more productive when they're rested and happy.

Work-from-home jobs are desirable for all the reasons stated but
many people who go searching for such positions have their lives turned
upside down by cybercriminals. In many cases, the bad guys target
people who are most vulnerable: those who are recently unemployed,
behind on their bills, fresh out of college, or caring for sick loved ones.
You've probably received hundreds of emails offering you an extra
$1,000 a week or a certain commission to handle financial transac-
tions from home. Or maybe you've seen similar job listings for "money
transfer agents," "local processors," "payment processing agents," and
other comparable titles on Craigslist or Monster.com. I receive these
emails all the time, and thankfully most of them end up in my spam
folder. Here's one example:

Dear friend,

   Greetings to you and your family, I am the manager of bill and
exchange in THE BANK, I have a business of 5.5 Million United State
Dollars to be transfer to your account for investment in your country,
if you are ready to assist get back to me, I will give you full details of
how the fund will be transfer to you.

   Be rest assured that everything will be handled confidentially
because, this is a great opportunity we cannot afford to miss, as
it will make our family profit a lot. 6 years ago, that most of the
greedy African Politicians used our bank to launder money overseas
through the help of their Political advisers most of the funds which
they transferred out of the shores of Africa were gold and oil money
that was supposed to have been used to develop the continent, as

I am sending this message to you, I was able to divert five point five Million Dollars ($5.5M) which is in an escrow transit account belonging to no one in the bank, and now my bank is very anxious to know the real beneficiary of the funds is for they have made a lot of profits with the fund.

Immediately the fund has been successfully transfer into your account I will come to your country for the sharing of the fund, the fund will be shared 50% for me and 40% for you, and the other 10% for the orphanages home and poor with less-privilege people.

Please indicate your interest in this transaction by replying back and if you are not interested do not waste your time to reply kindly delete my message from your box ok.

Waiting to hear from you soon.

Yours Faithfully,
Mrs. Elodie Azeez

Other than being a third-grade English teacher's worst nightmare, this email is a perfect example of a scam designed to lure you into becoming an online money mule for cybercriminals. I believe there's one simple rule to follow when you're searching for stay-at-home work: *If it's too good to be true, it probably is.* In every one of the business email compromise cases I investigated for the FBI, there was an easily identifiable victim, whether it was a company that had been scammed for millions of dollars or a retiree who lost his or her life savings. But, in some cases, there was another victim—a mule or unwitting accomplice who unknowingly assisted the bad guys in stealing money. Tragically, some of them were as much victims as the people who lost money.

Money mules perform an essential task for bad guys—they launder stolen money or merchandise and transfer it to cybercriminals who are usually located overseas. The mules are paid a flat fee or a certain percentage of the stolen funds for their services, and they're often stiffed or dropped after only one transaction. From January 2015 to June 2016, the FBI's Internet Crime Complaint Center said it received 22,143 complaints related to online money muling, totaling more than $3 billion in losses. Here's the really scary part: Money mules are complicit and risk criminal prosecution, even if they were *unknowingly* part of the scam. In many of the cases, however, the mules knew exactly what they were doing. In January 2018, a California woman was charged with acting as an intermediary in three email scams that stole more than $360,000 from three people in Minnesota, according to published reports. Federal authorities said the first email scam stole $205,704 from a home buyer; the second netted $90,000 from a woman who believed she was sending money to a woman involved in the gem industry in Dubai; and the third victim sent multiple deposits totaling $86,000 to a woman searching for love on Craigslist. Money mules are a worldwide problem. In November 2017, the U.S. assisted Europol and other European countries in Operation European Money Mule Action, which resulted in one hundred and fifty-nine arrests and fifty-nine money-mule organizers being identified.

Sadly, most of the money mules I interviewed while working for the FBI were unwitting accomplices in these scams. One such case involved a man we will call Drew, a disabled veteran of the Gulf War. The emotional and physical scars of the war took a heavy toll on Drew, who lost his job and family because of post-traumatic stress disorder. Once his wife and teenaged children left, Drew became an alcoholic and prescription pill abuser. He wasn't able to hold down a job and barely survived on his medical disability pension from the military. He finally sought help from a church and was slowly able to turn his life around through Alcoholics Anonymous and a lot of prayer. With his life seemingly back on track, Drew believed his prayers were answered when he responded to an employment listing on Craigslist. The job was a work-from-home position with flexible hours and no outside sales. The advertisement said the company was looking for someone with strong financial and communication skills. Drew had earned a bachelor's degree in finance through the GI Bill, and he believed the job was an opportunity he couldn't pass up. He replied to the job listing with his resume, and then he received an email from an individual who identified himself as Mr. Bart a few hours later.

Bart claimed to be the chief operating officer of a global company that was based in Ireland and allegedly purchased and sold high-priced commercial drilling equipment for oil exploration. Bart told Drew that the company was expanding into the Asia-Pacific Region and needed an executive in the U.S. who would work with vendors located around the world. Drew was told there was a training program, the hours were flexible, and he could work either part-time or full-time. His starting salary would be between $31.15 and $67.15 per hour depending on his skill level, and medical and retirement benefits were available to full-time employees. Drew felt like it was his lucky day; the job offer was the answer to his prayers. After Drew accepted the position, Bart directed him to open a commercial checking account in the name of Equipment Leasing Procurement International at a bank in the area where he lived. Once Drew opened the account, he sent the bank name and account and routing numbers to Bart. Over the next few days, Bart and Drew communicated via text messaging and Skype. Bart told Drew he would be getting new computer equipment and that it should be delivered within a few days.

Around 11:30 P.M. one night, Drew received a telephone call from Bart, who apologized for calling so late. It was 6:30 A.M. in Ireland, and Bart sounded stressed and frantic. He told Drew that the company had just located a hydraulic 9718 core-drill processor through a company in Hong Kong. Bart explained that a wire transfer of $5.5 million was coming to Drew's account, and he needed Drew to wire the money to a bank in Hong Kong as soon as his bank opened. When Drew arrived at his bank the next morning, he sat down with the branch manager, who seemed suspicious that so much money was being wired out of the country. The manager logged into his computer and saw that a $5.5 million wire transfer was indeed coming from another bank in the Midwest. When reached by phone, the manager at the other bank confirmed that the transaction was legitimate; she'd already contacted the controller of the company on the account, who said the money was for a large acquisition. The bank manager returned to Drew with a big smile and even offered to take him to lunch once the transaction was processed.

After leaving the bank, Drew sent a text message to Bart, informing him that the money had been wired to the bank in Hong Kong. Bart thanked Drew for doing a great job and promised that a big bonus would be in his account within a few hours. Drew couldn't believe how great the opportunity was turning out to be. For the first time in years, Drew felt like he was on top of the world. His life was getting better, and he decided he needed to go to church to thank God for all of his good fortune. At the same time, a cybercriminal in West Africa was probably jumping up and down and celebrating too. He'd probably just spoken to his colleague in Hong Kong, who confirmed that he'd received a $5.5 million wire transfer from an American bank. It was the type of score that would change a cybercriminal's life. After he distributed his partners' shares and most likely paid off more than a few bribes, this twenty-something cybercriminal would still be one of the richest men in his country. And, amazingly, it took very little effort and even less risk to pull off the heist.

A few weeks later, FBI agents visited Drew's house and interrogated him like a guy who was suspected of embezzling $5.5 million from a bank. Drew explained that he hadn't kept any of the money for himself— it had all been wired to a bank in Hong Kong. When an FBI agent asked Drew why he'd sent the money there, he told him he was only doing his job. The agent asked Drew why he didn't find it suspicious that his new job required him to send large amounts of money overseas—and why a company would entrust a new employee with so much responsibility. It took Drew only a few minutes to realize he'd participated in a $5.5 million scam and might face criminal prosecution. To make matters worse, the bank froze Drew's account and seized whatever money was still in it. Suddenly, his life didn't seem so rosy and had taken a turn for the worse.

A second type of work-at-home scam that I encountered often while working for the FBI targets college students, stay-at-home moms, and the elderly. The victim typically received an email, recruiting him or her as an accounts receivable clerk for a nonexistent company. These fake positions required the recipient to provide a bank account and routing number in order to receive outstanding bills from the supposed company. Once money was transferred into the account, the individual was instructed to wire transfer about 90 percent of the funds to another bank account or send it to the bad guys via Western Union. The individual received 10 percent of the funds as a commission, which seemed like a great job—at least until law enforcement knocked on the door. Where did the stolen money come from? In many cases, it was stolen from legitimate companies that weren't utilizing two-factor authentication. If a thief steals a username and password, he can break into the payroll software package and change the bank account and routing information. Instead of paying employees their salaries, the companies end up paying cybercriminals overseas. What better way for criminals to do it than with an army of unsuspecting college students and stay-at-home moms? By the time the company discovers that its employees haven't been paid and contacts the bank, it's too late to recover the money.

In another scam, the cybercriminals send fraudulent checks to mules and ask them to deposit them into their accounts. After taking a certain percentage of the money, the mules transfer the rest to the criminals' accounts. A few days later, the mules will learn the checks weren't real and that they actually sent *their own* money to the crooks.

Yet another online scam involving mules is the reshipper scheme, which involves shipping illegally obtained merchandise such as computers, TVs, and other expensive items to cybercriminals located overseas. The bad guys recruit mules through Craigslist, Monster.com, and other local message boards. They then direct their "new employees" to a company website, which looks like a legitimate shipping company. The victim will be asked to download an employment agreement, read it, and sign it. At that point, the recruit believes he or she is applying for an actual stay-at-home job. The employment agreement asks for the recruit's date of birth, Social Security number, and bank account and routing numbers. The mule is told that he or she will receive packages and that it's their job to open the boxes and inspect the items. Then they'll re-ship them to an address provided by the company, which are typically in West Africa and Eastern Europe. In a few days, computers and TVs that were purchased with stolen credit card numbers start arriving at the mule's home. Since most companies are suspicious when expensive merchandise is shipped to foreign countries, the mules serve as middlemen to prevent red flags. In some cases I investigated, the mules were paid with counterfeit checks; some of them were overpaid and even returned the overpayment with their own money before realizing their paycheck was fraudulent. In a nutshell, the victims lost a lot of money in the scams, and then law enforcement contacted them because thousands of dollars of stolen merchandise was shipped to their homes.

Monster.com, Craigslist, and other online job listings have made it so much easier for people to find stay-at-home jobs to supplement their income or work part-time while going to school or caring for loved ones. Unfortunately, the same technology has also made it easier for cybercrooks to create fraudulent positions to take advantage of them. It is crucial that you, as a job seeker, exercise common sense and caution when seeking online employment. Read position descriptions carefully and research companies before applying for jobs. Most importantly, remember this: If it sounds too good to be true, it's probably a scam.

HOW TO AVOID BECOMING A VICTIM

🔒 Follow one simple rule: *If the job sounds too good to be true, it probably is.*

🔒 Avoid stay-at-home job descriptions that include reshipping, accounts receivable, and billing clerk. They're usually scams.

🔒 Never accept a position that requires depositing money into your bank account and then wiring it to different accounts. In nearly every case, you'll be laundering stolen money for the bad guys.

🔒 If a job description includes poor use of the English language, including grammar, capitalization, and verb tenses, it's more than likely a scam. Many of the cybercriminals who send these types of emails aren't native English speakers.

🔒 Never provide credentials of any kind, such as bank account information, Social Security number, usernames, passwords, or any other personally identifiable information in response to a recruiting email.

🔒 Before accepting a position, ask for a job interview by phone, video-conference, or preferably in person. If the only job interview occurs via email or text messaging, it's probably a scam.

🔒 Research your potential employer before accepting a job. Search the Internet and other resources to determine whether or not you're interviewing with a legitimate company. Ask for its Web address and physical address. Check online business complaint sites, social media, and the Better Business Bureau.

CHAPTER 14

Finding Mr. or Mrs. Wrong

ONE OF THE MOST HEART-WRENCHING CASES I ENCOUNTERED
during my career with the FBI involved a woman in her late fifties,
divorced, and looking for love as she neared her golden years. It was
shortly after the Christmas holidays; Brooke was lonely, so she turned
to the Internet to find someone she could spend the rest of her life with.

In only a few short weeks, Brooke started communicating with a
man she knew as Anthony. He had supposedly attended Vanderbilt
University, studied chemical engineering, and then returned to his
native France to run his family's business. Anthony told Brooke that he
traveled the world for work and occasionally returned to the U.S. The
two talked on the phone, shared emails, and texted each other almost
every day for about eight months. They exchanged photographs and
tried to communicate several times via Skype or Facetime, but their
connections never worked. After months of correspondence, Brooke
fell in love with Anthony, and they made plans to build a dream house
together on the beach in Costa Rica. All Anthony needed to do was sell
his family estate in France and he would use the money to buy a vacation home they could share. Brooke would finally be able to have the
fairy-tale life she'd always dreamed about.

What prompted me to meet Brooke was a telephone call from her
attorney late one Friday night. The attorney advised me that Brooke
was the victim of cybercrime and had been defrauded by her online
boyfriend in France The first thing I told him was that it sounded like the
work of Nigerian bad guys, but he repeated to me that her boyfriend was
from France. There was a concerned tone in his voice that I'd heard too
many times before. I asked two important questions before he shared
details of her story:

1. How long ago was the money sent?
2. How much did she send?

The attorney said she'd wired $500,000 to an overseas account
about ten days earlier. I broke the bad news, which I'd shared with
hundreds of other cybercrime victims: it was too late to recover her

money, we're probably not going to be able to put the bad guys in jail, and this crime could have easily been prevented.

Millions of people around the world have turned to dating apps such as Tinder, OkCupid, Coffee Meets Bagel, and Match.com to find the perfect match, and more and more cybercriminals are preying on these good people. To get to your wallet, they'll first target your heart. The criminals' fake profiles are typically similar: They present themselves as white men in their late forties to sixties, say they attended American colleges, and claim to now be living overseas. This portrayal casts the crook as the lead character of a romance novel for their targets. The fake profiles usually contain a little intrigue, and the potential thieves try to show themselves as real, trusted people like military personnel, aid workers, or professionals working abroad. These fake Romeos never talk about sex, and they always seem to have a lot in common with their victims. It's easy to find similarities because there is plenty of information available about hobbies, background, and interests in their dating profiles. That's all the information the bad guys need in order to get to work.

In 2016, the FBI's Internet Crime Complaint Center received nearly fifteen thousand reports of *romance scams*, amounting to more than $230 million in losses. The U.S. states with the most victims were California, Florida, Texas, New York, and Pennsylvania. In some foreign countries, you'll find cybercriminals lined up in rows with computers, each one throwing out fishing lines in an attempt to land wealthy victims. In June 2018, the U.S. Attorney's Office for the Western District of New York announced that Adams Amen, a thirty-two-year-old citizen of Ghana living in Detroit, pleaded guilty to conspiracy to commit wire fraud. Between March 2015 and June 2017, the government alleged, Amen conspired with other Ghanaian nationals to devise an Internet romance scheme utilizing the dating website MillionaireMatch.com that netted them nearly $1 million from multiple victims. The cybercriminals made up fraudulent names and profiles or assumed someone else's identity. In this particular case, one of the victims received photographs of a man known to her as Marvin Roecker. The image was actually of a real estate agent from Texas who was *not* named Marvin Roecker, and who wasn't involved in the case at all.

Brooke was like a lot of the victims in romance scams, who are predominantly older women, divorced or widowed, computer-literate, and well educated. They are also emotionally vulnerable, and cyber-criminals know exactly how to tug at their heartstrings. The crook who targeted Brooke was an expert at his trade. I'm sure he spent hours polishing his skills and most likely kept a journal to better understand how to manipulate and exploit her. Since he was likely working on several potential victims at the same time, that journal was important; it's how he probably kept his lies straight. Brooke and Anthony communicated via the dating app for a few days, and then he suggested they chat more privately via text, telephone, and email. When I asked Brooke if she'd ever met Anthony in person, she said she'd talked to him almost every day. As you probably noticed, she didn't answer my question. When I asked her the question again, she replied that they were moving to Mexico together and going to live happily ever after. Brooke was a well-educated woman with a prominent position at a large company. But when she answered my questions about Anthony, she sounded like a delusional fifteen-year-old schoolgirl who was getting jerked around by her boyfriend.

Brooke told me that Anthony had arranged for her to receive a wire transfer of $500,000, which she was then supposed to wire to their homebuilder in Mexico. The request seemed absolutely legitimate to Brooke; Anthony was the love of her life, and she had no reason to doubt his intentions. On a Monday morning, Brooke received a text message from Anthony, confirming that $500,000 had been wired to her bank account. He added some urgency by telling her that the builder needed the money that same day so he could order the granite coun-tertops for her dream kitchen. Brooke left work and went to the bank to handle the transaction in person. She met with a manager who was happy to help her with the wire transfer. Brooke never kept more than $5,000 in her checking account, had never received such a large wire transfer, and had never wired money out of the country. But the branch manager never asked Brooke why she was sending such a large amount to a foreign country. For the most part, banks do an adequate job of educating customers and warning them about fraud. Even if this particular manager had advised Brooke that she might be involved in a scam, I think she probably wouldn't have believed him.

A few days after Brooke wired $500,000 to an overseas account, the originating bank that had allegedly transferred the proceeds from the sale of Anthony's family estate recalled the wire transfer. The money actually belonged to a title company in the U.S., which had been the victim of a business email compromise scam. Another cybercriminal had spoofed an email to the title company and directed someone there to send the proceeds from a real estate transaction to Brooke's account. Brooke was not only the victim of a romance scam, but the bank also considered her a suspect in an embezzlement scheme. Her life was turned upside down when she finally realized that Anthony wasn't real and that the man she thought she loved was a cybercriminal. The real financial victim in this case turned out to be the title company, which never recovered its money. But it was so painful for me to explain to a well-educated, adult woman that she had been scammed by a Nigerian cybercriminal.

When the title company's bank attempted to recall $500,000 from Brooke's bank, the money was already gone. However, the bank was able to seize $15,000, which was money that Brooke had earned and saved. When she attempted to recover her money from the other bank, however, she was told that she was also responsible for repayment of the remaining $485,000. Brooke was devastated and blamed herself for being so foolish. The psychological trauma suffered by victims is twofold: First they must cope with the end of what they believe is a serious romantic relationship; second, to compound the damage, they blame themselves (as do their family and friends).

In February 2017, the FBI shared another case of a romance scam victim who was courageous enough to share her story in hopes that other might avoid becoming victimized. Like Brooke, the woman was in her fifties. She lived in Texas and was in an emotionally abusive marriage. She met a man online, Charlie, who said he was the "friend of a friend." Charlie noticed that the woman was a strong Christian, which she openly publicized on her Facebook account. He told her that he was a Christian, too, and that he worked in the construction business in California. Over the next several months, they prayed and sang together on the phone and discussed church sermons on Sunday afternoons. After several months of correspondence, Charlie contacted her and said he needed $30,000 to finish a job. He promised to repay her the money in twenty-four to forty-eight hours. She prayed about his request and decided to wire him the money. She didn't hear from Charlie for a couple of days—until he requested an additional $30,000. Over the next two years, the woman ended up sending Charlie about $2 million. When her financial advisor noticed that her accounts were steadily dwindling, he contacted her and advised her to contact the FBI.

The FBI's investigation led to the arrest of two Nigerians posing as South African diplomats who traveled to the U.S. to collect money from her on Charlie's behalf. According to the FBI, Charlie claimed he was being paid $42 million for a construction project in South Africa, and she believed she was paying to have the money, including her $2 million, transferred to a bank in the U.S. In July 2016, the two Nigerian co-conspirators pleaded guilty for their roles in the scam, and a federal judge sentenced them each to thirty-six months in prison. Charlie is still on the loose, presumably in Nigeria, and might never be apprehended. The woman who was victimized told the FBI, "I not only invested money in this man, but there is a big, huge piece of my heart that I invested in him. It's not just the finances, it's the emotional part, too—being embarrassed, being ashamed, being humiliated." She continued, "I can't even imagine a man, a person, that could be this bad. I can't think of him that way. . . . There can't be a man in this world that could be this horrible to have purposefully done what he's done to me."

Unfortunately, there are thousands of men exactly like Charlie victimizing people around the world. But if you think women are the only victims of romance scams, think again. In 2017, Action Fraud, the cybercrime reporting center controlled by the City of London Police, reported that 39 percent of the romance-scam victims in that country were men. I've seen plenty of men fall victim to this scheme, and the details of the exchanges are fairly similar every time. The woman is generally much younger than her target and there always seems to be a lot of pillow talk and an exchange of intimate photographs. Many of these women claim to be from Eastern Europe, and they say they're looking for someone to marry and are willing to relocate to the U.S. That's when they start bleeding cash from the victims. They'll start by asking for a nice present. Before long, the victims are paying the woman's rent, sending her money for a plane ticket, and wiring her $10,000 for legal fees because she was arrested while trying to leave her native country.

Finding true love is difficult enough, and no one wants to be alone. That's what makes this type of cybercrime so emotionally painful for victims—and so profitable for criminals. The most important thing to remember about these types of schemes is that there is no *typical* victim. Targets can be male or female, young or old, straight or gay. The common denominator is that they're lonely and seeking a romantic relationship, and the bad guys are more than willing to take advantage of them.

HOW TO AVOID BECOMING A VICTIM

🔒 Research the person's photo and profile using online searches. If it's a scam, the same profile has probably been used before.

🔒 Go slowly and ask a lot of questions. You should also keep a journal and be prepared to identify inconsistencies.

🔒 Beware if an individual seems too perfect or knows too much about you.

🔒 Beware if an individual is attempting to isolate you from family and friends.

🔒 Beware if someone requests inappropriate photographs or financial information that could later be used to extort you.

🔒 If an individual promises to meet you in person but always comes up with an excuse why he or she can't, it's probably a scam. If you haven't met that person after a few months, for whatever reason, you have good reason to be suspicious.

🔒 If you agree to meet a prospective partner in person, make sure to tell family and friends who you're meeting and where you're going.

🔒 Never send money to someone you don't know personally. If you haven't met them in person, don't send them money.

🔒 Be cautious of people who portray themselves as military personnel, aid workers, and overseas workers. U.S. military officials say they receive thousands of complaints every year from scam victims around the world. Officials note military members will never need money for leave or healthcare, which are common requests made by cybercriminals.

🔒 Be alert to spelling and grammar mistakes, inconsistencies in their stories, and other signs that it's a scam.

🔒 Be careful about how much personal information you share on social media. Scammers use this type of information to create fake identities or target you in a scheme.

CHAPTER 15

Ramsomware

LET'S SAY YOU COME HOME FROM WORK ONE DAY AND LOG on to your computer, but you can't open any of your files. No matter what you do or how hard you try, you simply can't retrieve them. Regrettably, you realize that you've never backed up your important information, such as photographs, documents, music, videos, and contacts, and now it might be gone forever. Or maybe you did try to back it up recently but, for whatever reason, it didn't work. What if you'd been writing a thesis paper for months to complete your graduate degree? What if you were an author who had already written 80 percent of your next novel? What if you were a bookkeeper? A lawyer? A doctor? How much would you be willing to pay to get your clients' files back, instead of losing them forever? Would you pay $200? Or maybe $500? Or even $1,000? What if you found yourself in this quandary and were suddenly presented with a solution and opportunity to get all of your stuff back? It sounds like a great business decision—especially for the bad guys who are holding your information hostage.

Encryption has been a wonderful thing in the digital world. It was designed to keep our computers safe, so, as long as your information was encrypted, any would-be thieves who found your laptop (or stole it) wouldn't be able to gain access. Unless your password is extremely weak, such as jordan2005 or password123, a bad guy would probably have a difficult time accessing your files. As a result, cybercriminals figured out a way to subvert the value of encryption and use it *against* you to make money. Hackers created what we now call ransomware; you may have heard of some recent examples, such as the Cryptolocker virus, CryptoWall, Locky, Cerber, KeyRanger, SamSam, TeslaCrypt, TorrentLocker, and Reveton. Ransomware is a type of malware that targets both human and technical weaknesses in an effort to block users from accessing important data and/or systems—until the victim pays a ransom in exchange for a decryption key that unlocks the captive files and/or system.

Here's how ransomware works: You log in to your computer and can't access any of the information. After you figure out that you can't remove a nasty virus to open your files, you'll find a note in your system that says something like, "Hi, my name is Boris Badenov. If you don't pay me $500 in bitcoin in the next twenty-four hours, you'll never get your information back." You, like most people, may not even know that bitcoin is untraceable virtual electronic currency. Because Boris is so nice, he has presented you with a low-cost solution that will allow you to retrieve your files. It's like he's giving you a magic wand to make the nightmare go away, right?

How did you get ransomware on your computer? You most likely received a spear-phished email with a link, and when you clicked the link you were taken to a website where the malicious payload was installed. There's a good chance there was a vulnerability in one of your software programs, and either you didn't patch the program or the crooks discovered it before the vendor did. Once a malicious payload is installed on your computer, it locates all of your important files—documents, photos, videos, databases, and music. The ransomware is designed to encrypt all of that information and lock you out; some variations of ransomware even impact your operating system and prevent the computer from starting. The encryption is sophisticated and usually unbreakable; a super computer at a university isn't even powerful enough to defeat it. Ransomware can be especially damaging to your computer at work, which is probably connected to a network. If the network is poorly configured, the infection can spread through an entire organization.

In my opinion—based on more than twenty years of investigating these types of crimes for the FBI—only a small percentage of these sorts of losses are ever reported to law enforcement because of embarrassment and fear of reputational damage. I have witnessed cases like these play out on an almost daily basis. Large organizations are getting better at recovering from these incidents, but more homeowners and small businesses are becoming victims of ransomware all the time. In 2017, for example, the FBI's Internet Crime Complaint Center reported receiving 1,783 complaints identified as ransomware, with losses totaling more than $2.3 million. Those were only the cases that were actually *reported* to the FBI. Some cybersecurity firms have suggested that the number of ransomware attacks worldwide might be closer to seven hundred thousand or more annually, and Cybersecurity

Ventures predicts ransomware damages will climb to $11.5 billion glob-
ally by 2019. Ransom demands are typically between $500 and $1,000
for each individual attack; the data-kidnappers generally ask for lowish
ransoms so more will be paid. However, some ransoms have been much
more expensive for larger companies. I had one company call me and
say it paid $28,000 in ransom but still didn't receive the decryption keys.
In 2017, South Korean web provider Nayana paid three hundred and
ninety-seven bitcoin—about $1 million U.S. at the time—to unlock more
than three thousand four hundred websites that were encrypted with
ransomware. At the time, it was the single largest-known payout for a
ransomware attack.

If you hadn't heard of ransomware before, you probably learned
about it on May 17, 2017, when the WannaCry ransomware was
released. It infected computers and networks around the world, and it
certainly made a lot of people want to cry. WannaCry infected Windows
computers with a worm that encrypted files on the hard drives and
made them impossible for users to access. The attackers took advantage of a flaw in Microsoft that had previously been detected by the
National Security Agency. Microsoft released a patch to prevent pene-
tration, and anyone who updated a system had nothing to worry about.
Of course, not everyone downloaded and installed the patch.

WannaCry infected about two hundred thousand computers in one
hundred and fifty countries around the world; the four most affected
were Russia, Ukraine, India, and Taiwan. One of the largest single agencies impacted by the attack was the National Health Services network
of hospitals in England and Scotland—as many as seventy thousand
devices, including computers, MRI scanners, and blood-storage refrigerators were infected. Large companies such as Honda, Hitachi, Nissan,
Renault, FedEx, Deutsche Bank, and LG Electronics, as well as universities in Colombia, Greece, Italy, and China, also reported their networks
were infected with WannaCry. Even governments weren't immune from
the ransomware; the Russian Ministry of Internal Affairs, Chinese public
security bureau, and state governments in India were also targeted. It
was estimated that WannaCry caused $4 billion in damage and ransom
worldwide.

Healthcare providers in particular are targeted most often because their patients' information is so critical to operations and so sensitive in nature. In February 2016, a hacker attacked computer systems at Hollywood Presbyterian Medical Center near Los Angeles. The hospital paid a $17,000 ransom in bitcoin to obtain a decryption key; it disputed an earlier report that hackers wanted $3.4 million. In March 2016, cybercriminals infected more than nine thousand machines at Ottawa Hospital in Canada, but the hospital was able to wipe the drives and recover files from backups.

Public agencies and critical infrastructure, including transportation and utilities, are also popular targets of ransomware. In November 2016, computer systems at San Francisco's transit system, Muni, were attacked. The cybercriminals wanted $73,000 as ransom, but the transit authority refused to pay and restored its system in two days. It still suffered significant losses, though, because riders were allowed to ride for free during the two days the computer system was down.

When I receive a call from ransomware victims, I tell them they're going to be okay as long as they have a good recent backup. In most cases, there's dead silence on the other end. If I don't hear a word for three or four seconds, I pretty much know they don't have a recent backup in place. Sending bad guys money for a decryption key should really be called "pay and pray," because what you're doing is paying a ransom and then praying you'll get your stuff back. I've had cases in which victims paid and still didn't get their money back, and others in which victims paid and then the crooks asked for even more money. Like the saying goes, there's no honor among thieves. I try to explain to victims that it's never a good idea to pay ransom; it only keeps them in business. Even worse, the money you pay them not only supports criminal organizations but maybe even terrorist groups. As I've said a few times already, a good backup of your data can save you a world of heartache.

To be clear, the FBI *does not support* paying ransom to cybercriminals. In its 2017 Internet Crime Report, the FBI described its policy about ransomware:

Paying a ransom does not guarantee an organization will regain access to their data; in fact, some individuals or organizations were never provided with decryption keys after having paid a ransom. Paying a ransom emboldens the adversary to target other organizations for profit and provides for a lucrative environment for other criminals to become involved. While the FBI does not support paying a ransom, there is an understanding that when businesses are faced with an inability to function, executives will evaluate all options to protect their shareholders, employees, and customers.

I couldn't have said it better myself.

How long can a business survive without access to its network or records? Not for very long. I remember receiving a call from the owner of a small accounting firm who called me in a panic when his files were held hostage. His firm's IT company had been trying to retrieve his data for a month. To make matters worse, it was April 14—the day before the federal tax deadline. The hackers had frozen the firm's work from the previous month. The owner of the accounting firm made the best case I've ever heard for paying ransom. "If I don't pay the $500," he told me, "then I will lose approximately $150,000 in billable work, and I'll go out of business." I wished him luck and told him I'd pray for him. Like I said, when you pay the ransom, you usually don't get your stuff back.

Sometimes the bad guys have no intention of unlocking your data, and other times the encryption keys are lost forever. Cybercriminals don't like to keep incriminating evidence on their own computers, so they'll often hide encryption keys on other people's computers—the ones they've already hacked. Every so often, a company discovers that bad guys are using its computers and immediately takes them offline. When that happens, the victims who paid ransom for encryption keys might be out of luck because the cybercrooks can't access the keys even if they wanted to.

Like most cybercrime, identifying and apprehending the criminals behind ransomware is never easy. In one of my FBI investigations, a criminal who developed a specific variant of ransomware was indicted by the U.S. Attorney's Office. The problem was that he lived in Russia, and the Russian government doesn't cooperate with the U.S. when we want to arrest one of its citizens for computer intrusion.

Nonetheless, the FBI and other international law enforcement agencies are certainly trying to stop the bad guys behind ransomware. In December 2017, the FBI and UK National Crime Agency, along with Romanian and Dutch investigators, arrested five individuals in Romania who were suspected of spreading two major ransomware variants—CTB-Locker and Cerber. Google's research estimated that Cerber had generated about $6.9 million before it was stopped. Two of the suspects arrested, a twenty-five-year-old man and twenty-eight-year-old woman, were also suspected of illegally accessing one hundred and twenty-three computers that help run the Washington D.C. Metropolitan Police Department's surveillance cameras. Not coincidentally, this happened just ahead of President Donald Trump's inauguration in January 2017. Remember what I said earlier? These hackers aren't teenaged kids sitting in front of computers in their parents' basements. They're intelligent, sophisticated hackers who have unfortunately decided to use their skills to commit major crimes.

What's the best way to back up your data? The first and most important step is to identify your mission-critical information. If you're working on a thesis paper or bestselling novel and haven't made backup copies, you're at great risk. The same goes for tax records, accounting spreadsheets, and other important business documents. You can always reinstall software programs and maybe retrieve music, but some things are too valuable to lose. Think about it for a while, and then go to your computer and open your files. A lot of people prefer to store their most important documents in free cloud-based accounts like Google Drive, Microsoft's OneDrive, Apple's iCloud, or Dropbox. But keeping a copy in the cloud without two-factor authentication is just asking for trouble, in my opinion.

The best thing to do is to go out and purchase a portable USB hard drive; a 1 TB drive costs about $60. Then copy your files from the computer to the external hard drive either manually or using one of the many available software backup options. At that point, you'll have a complete backup for your most important documents. When the backup is complete—and this is important—unplug the drive from your computer and put it in a safe place. Then set up a schedule and back up your data accordingly, whether it's daily, weekly, or monthly, or whatever fits your needs.

Now, what if there is a fire in your house and both your computer *and* the backup drive are destroyed? You can purchase a fireproof box and hope it makes it through a fire or that it will survive a tornado or a flood. Another option is to use a paid online backup service, such as Amazon Cloud Services or Carbonite. Find one that supports most of your devices and use the downloadable app provided to make a mirror image of your files. The *best* option is to do both: Back up locally on a hard drive you can keep safe *and* back up to a cloud storage provider that keeps your data safely offsite. As many security professionals say, if you don't have at least three copies of your data, your data isn't *really* backed up at all.

There is nothing worse technologically than not having your important information backed up or realizing that your computer has been infected with ransomware, leaving you no choice but to pay and pray that you'll get your stuff back. Don't let Boris steal or encrypt your only copy of your important files. Get a backup strategy in place today.

HOW TO AVOID BECOMING A VICTIM

🔒 Identify your most important data and regularly back it up, always verifying the integrity of those backups. Backups are critical in ransomware attacks. If you are infected, your backups might be the only way to recover your critical data.

🔒 Secure your backups. Make sure they're not connected to the computers or networks they're backing up. Secure backups on the cloud or physically store them offline on external hard drives.

🔒 One backup is never enough, so make sure to use a cloud-based backup system, as well as an external hard drive to be especially safe. Be sure to use a cloud service that offers two-factor authentication—and turn that feature on immediately.

🔒 Patch your operating system and set up regular and automatic updates. Ransomware writers are constantly writing new variants and strains, and software vendors regularly offer patches and updates to protect systems from new ransomware.

🔒 Make sure your browser is also up to date, whether it's Microsoft Edge, Google Chrome, Firefox, Safari, Opera, or anything else. They all have vulnerabilities that are being patched all the time.

🔒 Be certain that you have a reputable antivirus security suite and firewall installed on your computer. The antivirus software will help you identify threats or suspicious behavior.

🔒 Most importantly, as always, think before you click a link or open an attachment. Practice your human firewall skills. Most ransomware is installed when the victim clicks a link or opens an attachment.

🔒 Employ content scanning and filtering on your email servers. Incoming email should be scanned for known threats and block any attachments that might pose a threat.

🔒 If you fear your computer has been infected, immediately disconnect it from your network and disable Wi-Fi and Bluetooth to prevent the malware from spreading to other machines.

🔒 Don't pay ransom to the hackers. Studies show that hackers still fail to decrypt the victims' data one of out of every four times, despite being paid. Remember that paying the bad guys only encourages them and funds their illegal operation.

CHAPTER 16

Better Online Banking

ALMOST A DECADE AGO, WHEN I WAS STILL WORKING FOR the FBI, I received a telephone call from an attorney. And, like almost everyone else who called me back then, there was desperation in his voice. He had discovered that $500,000 had been wired without his consent to an account at Alpha Bank in Moscow. The escrow account contained his client's money, and his bank informed him that it couldn't recall an overseas wire transfer. I told him that recalling an international wire is next to impossible, but we'd do everything possible to try and help him.

We had FBI agents working in Moscow, but we were getting very little help from the Russian government at the time. We discovered that the bad guys had installed a keystroke logger that had given them access to the attorney's bank account. Today, the controls employed at most banks are much more robust, which makes it more arduous for cyber-criminals to send international wire transfers, but it's still easy for them to gain access to bank accounts and send domestic wire transfers and ACH transfers (electronic checks). By the end of our investigation, the attorney managed to recover approximately $450,000, losing $50,000 through the debacle. In this case, he discovered the wire transfer imme-diately, and the transfer fortunately occurred when banks were closed in Moscow. It was a lucky break that I rarely saw in my career. He was agitated about losing some of his client's money, but I told him it was one of the luckiest days of his life. He looked at me with a puzzled expression. "How can you say that?" he asked. "I just lost $50,000." I explained how close he'd come to losing $500,000 and told him to take his wife to an expensive restaurant to celebrate. He was the exception when it comes to recovering stolen money, there's no question about it. In my whole career, I probably only had four or five cases in which the victims actually recovered their money.

Of course, the entire ordeal might have been prevented if the attorney had used two-factor authentication on his commercial bank accounts. Most people don't know it, but commercial accounts are not afforded the same protection as consumer accounts. If cybercriminals gain access to your personal account and steal your money, there's a good chance you're going to be reimbursed because the Federal Deposit

Insurance Corporation (FDIC) guarantees your deposits and your bank will probably be liable for any losses. However, if a hacker gains access to your business account, you're probably going to be out of luck in getting your money back. Some of the losses suffered by small businesses during the past few years have been sizable. According to the FDIC, a car dealer in Abilene, Kansas, lost $63,000 after its business manager's computer was infected with malware, which allowed cybercriminals to initiate payroll for nine fictitious employees. A construction company in Sanford, Maine, lost $345,444 (more than $500,000 was taken) because of malware, and an escrow group in Huntington Beach, California, was forced to close after bad guys walked away with roughly $1.5 million. I wonder how many of those business owners were aware they were at such risk.

Anyone who maintains a commercial account needs to be aware of this little-known fact: Personal and business accounts are governed by different rules and restrictions. Personal accounts are governed under Federal Reserve Regulation E (12 C.F.R. Part 205), which ensures coverage and reimbursement for lost funds due to fraudulent activity. The Uniform Commercial Code covers commercial accounts, and certain banks' policies are typically much less generous to account holders in the event of fraud. In most instances, the burden is on the business owner to notify the bank immediately if there is a disputed transaction, sometimes in as little as twenty-four hours, depending on a bank's policies. Unless you have a long-standing relationship with your bank, it might not be cooperative about returning your money; and, of course, many of the smaller banks aren't financially capable of giving it back. Most customers expect to be made whole when they are victims of credit card and ATM fraud, but some have been forced to sue smaller banks to recover bigger losses because their banks blamed them for allowing the cybercrime to happen.

I was the bearer of this bad news to dozens of businesses that were victimized this way. Large businesses always seem to recover and manage to survive after suffering a loss, but I witnessed numerous instances in which smaller businesses were forced to close their doors after being victimized by cybercriminals. It still breaks my heart because it doesn't *have* to happen. Cyber-liability insurance won't save you when your commercial checking account is cleaned out, nor will the FDIC or identity theft protection services such as LifeLock. If I had the money, I'd purchase advertising time during the Super Bowl to educate the country about this.

If you have commercial bank accounts, the first thing you need to do is make sure to enable two-factor authentication, which will prevent the thieves from breaking in. People tell me all the time that their bank doesn't offer 2FA. Remember what I told you about email providers that didn't offer it? As an FBI agent, I wasn't supposed to provide advice, but there were times when I took off my FBI hat and offered suggestions. If my bank didn't offer 2FA for commercial accounts, I'd go shopping for another bank. The website www.twofactorauth.org is a great resource to find out which banks offer two-factor authentication. Most of the larger banks are more technologically advanced because they have the money to spend on software, app developers, and security teams. Some of the smaller banks and credit unions simply can't afford those levels of protection, even though keeping their clients' money secure should be paramount.

Now, as a private citizen, I'm free to offer whatever suggestions I think may help. For instance, if you can afford it, I suggest you purchase a separate computer for online banking. Hopefully, the attorney who nearly lost $500,000 of his client's money did exactly that the next day. Most cybercrime occurs because someone clicks a link, opens an attachment they should have ignored, or goes to a website that installs malicious code. If you take away those threats, you're seriously reducing your risk when it comes to cybercrime. It's such a simple solution, really.

But what if the cybercrooks infect another computer on your network? They can still infect a properly protected computer that's networked to a compromised one. To avoid that, you could purchase a mobile hotspot device, such as Verizon's Jetpack or AT&T's Nighthawk mobile hotspot router. Only connect the computer you're using for banking to that particular network, and you can also use it when you're traveling. At its most basic level, this is called *application whitelisting* or *network segmentation*. Application whitelisting only permits allowed applications to be present and active on a computer system, and, in this case, the computer would only be used for banking purposes. Under no circumstances should you surf the Internet or check email from it. That means no Facebook, Twitter, or Instagram either. Making occasional exceptions, as tempting as they might be, would undermine the entire purpose of this approach.

I receive mixed reactions when I preach this point at nearly every one of my cybercrime prevention seminars. Organizations are never keen on change, especially when changes cost them money and slow down the business process. Everybody wants access to a multipurpose device that can surf the web, check email, play games, watch videos, and engage in mission-critical banking. But, if I were handling millions of dollars for my clients—or even thousands of dollars for smaller companies—I would seriously consider this approach as a safeguard.

A few years ago, I met with representatives of an organization that earned about $300 million annually, and we dissected its most mission-critical asset: its bank account—or, more specifically, its *access* to its bank account. The company had an information technology manager whose sole responsibility was to ensure the company's technology operated effectively and efficiently. I asked him a series of questions and discovered that the company didn't utilize two-factor authentication and didn't have a designated computer for banking. At the conclusion of my meeting, I had an in-depth briefing with the company's executives and brought up my concerns. They explained that their bank didn't offer two-factor authentication, but they didn't want to change banks because they had a long-standing relationship. When I addressed the issue of not having a designated computer for banking, the company's chief financial officer complained that he didn't like the idea of having two computers on his desk. In the end, the company decided it would take its chances with its current setup. When the meeting was over, one of the executives asked me a question that I hear all the time, "Why would anyone want to target us? We're not a large company." Remarkably, he was talking about a company that earns $300 million per year.

Another question I hear at conferences all the time involves bank apps for mobile devices. More and more, Americans are avoiding the long lines at banks and credit unions for the convenience of online and mobile banking. According to the Federal Financial Institutions Examination Council, the number of commercial banks and savings institutions decreased from 13,401 in 1988 to 4,852 at the end of the first quarter of 2018. Why? It's because everyone is replacing traditional banking with online and mobile banking. While Americans are abandoning brick-and-mortar banks for their smartphones and computers, reports suggest that most still have security-related concerns when using online and mobile banking. And there's legitimate reason for concern when we can do everything from paying our bills to depositing checks on mobile devices.

So, are bank apps safe? A few years ago, I was speaking at a big conference in Nashville, Tennessee, and the audience consisted of bank executives from around the country. I asked the audience how many of their banks offered apps, and almost everyone in the ballroom raised their hands. Then I asked, "Do any of your banks have an IT guy on staff who developed the app?" No one raised his or her hand. Banks don't write apps; they have somebody else write them for them. Then I asked the question that people ask me all the time, "Are bank apps safe?" I looked out into the audience and everyone was staring back at me. It was dead silence. I said, "Come on guys, it's either safe or it's not." Again, dead silence. So, I asked, "What if I was your customer? What would you say to me?" Still nothing, and, boy, was I losing my audience with that question. I finally said, "That's why I'm here today. I found out that the answer is *no*." I told a white lie to the bankers and claimed to have tracked down a guy in the Ukraine who developed a lot of their apps. I joked that I thought I'd heard him say, "Yes, bank apps are safe," or maybe he said, "Nyet," which is Russian for *no*.

I use this story a lot because we don't know who is writing the bank apps—or any other apps, for that matter—that we use every single day. Have we vetted the developers to make sure they're good guys and not Boris Badenov's first cousin? And, even if they are good guys and can be trusted, how secure are the apps they've created? Did they use a security framework to test the app and make sure it was safe? Or, did they just bring it to market as quickly as possible to get paid? Like a lot of other things involving the Internet, it's all about having faith. Do I use my bank's app? Yes, I do. As I told you earlier, I'm not willing to move in with the Eskimos.

So, for argument's sake, let's assume your bank app is 100 percent safe. That's great—as long as you don't have any other apps on your smartphone. Apps are here to stay, and we'll continue to download them, install them, and run them on our phones to play games, read email, watch live sporting events, listen to music, and do just about anything else. But I'm worried that apps are the newest attack vector for the bad guys. They realize how much we use apps, and I'm sure they're developing countless ways to penetrate deficiencies in them. I honestly believe apps are the future of cybercrime, and that scares the heck out of me. In 2018, there were 3.5 million apps for Android users and 2.1 million in the Apple App Store. If you believe every one of them is safe and secure, I've got some Enron stock I'd like to sell you. Remember, the biggest threat in online and mobile banking comes from using a compromised device, one with malware that steals a username and password. So think long and hard about what you're doing before you download and install another app on your phone. Every app you add alongside your banking app is one more opportunity to get hacked.

Many years later, I bumped into the lawyer who lost $50,000 of his client's money to a bank in Moscow. He told he purchased a second computer the next day—and that it was the best decision he'd ever made.

HOW TO AVOID BECOMING A VICTIM

🔒 Be aware of your bank's policy for reporting fraud, including timelines and reporting requirements, which could be as few as twenty-four hours for commercial accounts.

🔒 Purchase a separate computer for online banking and don't use it for any other purpose—period.

🔒 Equip your computers with up-to-date antivirus software and firewalls to block unwanted access.

🔒 Educate your employees about the dangers of clicking on unsolicited email and attachments. The website www.BusinessIDtheft.org is a great resource for educational materials, resources, and tips on preventing theft and fraud.

🔒 Restrict employees' use of computers for non-business activities, such as social media, e-commerce, and Web surfing.

🔒 Never access bank websites or mobile apps through public Wi-Fi in places like coffee shops, airports, or hotels. Those networks aren't secure and are extremely vulnerable to cybercrime.

🔒 Before downloading any bank app from your phone's app store, pay close attention to the name of the app provider or source in the app store description. Be sure you're actually downloading the bank's real app and not a cybercrook's lookalike. Cybercriminals will create lookalike fake apps to steal your login credentials and account and routing numbers.

🔒 Make sure your mobile devices require a password or biometric authentication, such as a fingerprint, for logging in. That will make it more difficult for criminals to access your phone if it's lost or stolen.

🔒 Be sure to log out of your bank's website or app after using it. Leaving them open will make it easier to access if your device is lost or stolen.

🔒 Set up fraud alerts through email, text messaging, or your bank's app, which can help alert you to suspicious or fraudulent activity.

🔒 Monitor and reconcile your bank account balances and transactions daily to report suspicious and fraudulent transactions immediately.

🔒 Consider using credit cards rather than commercial bank accounts for business expenses. Some credit cards offer more generous protections in regards to fraud and theft.

🔒 Review your company's general liability insurance policy and determine if it's covered for loss due to bank fraud. If it's not, contact your insurance agent to find a policy that offers it.

CHAPTER 17

Elder Scams

THE ELDERLY ARE AMONG OUR MOST VULNERABLE CITIZENS, and (not surprisingly) they're among those who are most often targeted by cybercriminals. There were nearly fifty thousand complaints of fraud involving victims over the age of sixty reported to the Federal Bureau of Investigation in 2017, with adjusted losses totaling more than $342 million. The U.S. Government Accountability Office estimated in 2018 that financial fraud targeting older Americans probably cost seniors about $2.9 billion annually. Most fraud, they say, isn't reported because either the victims don't know *where* to report it, they're too ashamed to admit they've been scammed, or they *don't even know* they've been victimized.

On February 22, 2018, U.S. Attorney General Jeff Sessions announced the formation of the Elder Justice Initiative, which is designed to support and coordinate the U.S. Department of Justice's enforcement efforts to combat elder abuse, neglect, and financial frauds and scams that target senior citizens. "The Justice Department and its partners are taking unprecedented, coordinated action to protect elderly Americans from financial threats, both foreign and domestic," Sessions said at the time. "When criminals steal the hard-earned life savings of older Americans, we will respond with the tools at the Department's disposal—criminal prosecutions to punish offenders, civil injunctions to shut the schemes down, and asset forfeiture to take back ill-gotten gains."

The Elder Justice Initiative seeks to provide targeted training and resources to prosecutors, law enforcement, judges, victim specialists, first responders, and civil legal aid employees to better respond to elder abuse. The U.S. Senate Special Committee on Aging is also working hard to educate elderly citizens and their families about the dangers of telephone and computer scams. The bad guys use a variety of scams to target senior citizens, including impersonating agents of the Internal Revenue Service or telling them they've won millions of dollars in the Jamaican lottery (but need to send money to claim their prize).

Some schemes originate over the Internet, while others are conducted by telephone. I once received a call about an incident involving a man named Martin, an eighty-year-old retired attorney. One night, Martin received a phone call and the muffled voice on the other end sounded like his grandson, Fred. "Grandpa, I'm in trouble and need your help," the man said. Martin asked Fred what was wrong and how he could help. Fred explained that he was in Florida for spring break, and his taxi driver had been arrested for having drugs in the trunk of his car. The police accused Fred of being an accomplice and arrested him too. Unless Fred paid $2,500 in bond, the police were going to keep him in jail until a trial two weeks later. Martin knew his grandson was indeed on vacation in Florida for spring break and started to worry. Fred begged his grandfather not to tell his parents, because they'd get angry if they knew he was in trouble. Fred was studying at Vanderbilt University, and he told his grandfather that he had a final exam the following week and would fail the course if he missed it.

Martin would do anything for his family—especially his grandson, whom he loved dearly. Martin asked Fred if he needed an attorney, and he replied that he only needed bail money and had already located a bail bondsman. After Martin agreed to send the money, Fred put him on the phone with a bail bondsman, who provided him with instructions on how to send the money via Western Union. The bail bondsman also told Martin that police had confiscated Fred's cell phone as evidence, so he provided him with another phone number to call once the money was wired. Later that night, Martin went to a Western Union location and wired $2,500 to the bondsman. A few hours later, he received another phone call from Fred asking for an additional $2,500 to pay a fine, and he went back to Western Union to wire more money.

Fortunately, during Martin's second visit, the Western Union clerk asked him why he was sending the money. Martin explained that his grandson was in jail and needed help. The clerk asked why Fred's parents weren't sending the money, and he explained that he was trying to cover for his grandson. At this point, the Western Union clerk was concerned that the elderly man might be a victim of a scam. Together, they called Fred's cell phone. Fred answered and said, "Hi, Grandpa. How are you?" Martin asked him if he'd been released from jail yet, and Fred sounded confused. Fred replied that he hadn't been in jail and was perfectly fine.

By the time Martin contacted me, it was too late to get his money back. It was long gone. It's extremely difficult to track money sent through the Western Union network since the recipient can pick it up at any location around the world. It didn't take long to figure out what happened either. The bad guys were able to view Fred's Facebook profile since he had set it to public (meaning anyone could view his posts). There, they identified his family and friends and saw photographs from his vacation in Florida. When they researched Martin, they discovered he was Fred's grandfather, worked as an attorney, and lived in an expensive part of town. All that information is easily accessible through county tax records and professional licensing, which are available to anyone online. Since Martin was eighty years old, the thief took a gamble by muffling his voice and pretending to be Fred. If the bad guys had asked for $10,000 or $20,000 for bail money, I'm pretty sure Martin would have paid it. He was willing to do anything to help his beloved grandson.

Grandparents are an easy target for cybercriminals. The crooks prey on the elders' love for their family and, oftentimes, their limited knowledge of Internet scams. I've seen grandparents be targeted by a bad guy who claimed that their loved ones had been involved in a car wreck and needed money for towing and medical bills. The messages are always sent with a sense of urgency, and the thieves allege that not sending the money will cause even more harm to their endangered family members. Thinking about this particular scenario doesn't just break my heart, it makes my blood boil.

I recently met a woman at a cybercrime prevention conference who explained that her daughter was traveling to South America for a mission trip. Her daughter had shared that news with the entire world on her Facebook account, and her mother wanted to know what she should do about it since it was already too late to delete the information on Facebook. I told her to expect telephone calls and emails from cybercriminals pretending to be her daughter, claiming to be in trouble, and asking for money. We can't control what the crooks are going to do, but we *can* control how we react. I told the woman to establish a predetermined code word that only she and daughter knew in case she was really in trouble. They could also come up with a series of questions that no one else would be able to answer. I told her to make sure they didn't discuss the code word or questions and answers over text messaging and email. And, of course, I encouraged her to tell her daughter to quit sharing details of her personal life on social media. We make it so easy for the bad guys to victimize us sometimes.

One of the most rapidly growing scams involving the elderly is computer tech-support scams, in which cybercriminals pose as representatives of well-known companies—such as Apple, Microsoft, McAfee, Norton, or Dell—and advise victims that their computers have been infected with a virus. The bad guys will attempt to gain access to a victim's computer remotely so they can steal personal information and other files, or they'll inject malware into the computer that the victim would have to pay to remove. Then they'll obtain credit card or bank account and routing numbers to bill the victims for their so-called "computer services."

The cybercriminals typically call the victims on the telephone, offering to "clean" their computers or remove a virus they're about to install. They'll ask for $500 to $1,000 for subscriptions to anti-virus software, and they'll even offer "senior citizen discounts" if the victim complains that the price is too high. In other cases, victims have called a telephone number that appears in a pop-up window on their computer screen. Scammers have used the pop-up windows to hack into victims' computers or lock them out and demand ransom. The Federal Trade Commission also discovered that cybercrime networks have been spending millions of dollars to advertise their fraudulent services through Google and other search engines. The search terms include words like *virus removal, McAfee Customer Support,* and *Norton Support.* The search-engine keywords are carefully chosen to confuse victims into believing the criminals are offering legitimate services from trusted band names. Even if they're selling you actual software, it's probably nothing you really need. Cybercriminals have also been known to call victims back weeks later to offer them refunds on their contracts. The bad guys will obtain the victims' bank account records to allegedly send them a refund—but then use their banking information to steal money from them again. I'm telling you, cybercriminals must have a reserved room in hell.

My friend's mom was surfing the Internet one evening when a blue screen popped up on her computer with a warning that looked authentic. The message on the screen said that her computer was infected with a serious virus and she needed to act immediately because her antivirus software had expired. If she didn't act right away, the message warned her, she'd lose all of her data. When my friend spoke to his mother, she was very concerned. The message instructed her to click a link to go to a website where she could use her credit card to pay $79 for an update to her antivirus software. Thankfully, she picked up the phone and called her son before using her credit card. My friend advised her that the blue screen was a scam, and he instructed her to shut down her computer, unplug it, then plug it back in and start it up. Once the computer turned back on, the blue screen was gone. The scam is called a *fake antivirus attack*, and it has been around for about a decade. It is still going strong because unsophisticated computer users enter the market everyday. Once the victim provides his or her credit card number to the bad guys, another screen pops on the computer that says the virus has been removed, and the computer is now functioning properly. In reality, the only thing the victim has done is given the bad guys a credit card number to use unlawfully.

Computer tech-support fraud is a huge business around the world. In May 2018, the U.S. Department of Justice announced that it had arrested two Florida men who allegedly owned and operated two tech-support scam companies: Client Care Experts, LLC, based in Boynton Beach, Florida, and ABC Repair Tech, based in Costa Rica. From approximately November 12, 2013, until at least December 9, 2016, the federal government alleges, the two men and others conspired to defraud more than forty thousand people across the U.S. and other foreign countries. These criminals raked in more than $25 million, according to prosecutors, by purchasing pop-up ads that appeared without warning on consumers' computer screens and locked up their browsers. The pop-ups falsely told users that their computers were infected with malware and viruses and that they were in danger of losing their data. Just as my friend's mother saw on her screen, the ads instructed them to call a toll-free number for help.

Computer users should be extremely careful whenever a screen pops up on a computer claiming they have a virus. The pop-ups trick the users into clicking a link, and by now you hopefully know what happens when you click on an unfamiliar link. It will usually get you into trouble, because the link is designed to install malware that either steals your password and username or encrypts all of your files so they can't be unlocked without paying a ransom. That's a horrible trap for anyone to fall into—especially our nation's seniors.

HOW TO AVOID BECOMING A VICTIM

🔒 Do not give remote control of your computer to a salesperson or technician who calls you unannounced.

🔒 If you receive an urgent or unscheduled call from someone who claims to be tech support, hang up the phone. Ninety-nine out of one hundred times, it's going to be a scammer.

🔒 Do not rely on caller ID to authenticate the person on the other end of the phone. Cybercriminals spoof caller ID numbers or block their numbers before contacting victims. They can make it appear they're calling from Microsoft or Apple, but they might really be located in West Africa or Eastern Europe.

🔒 Remember that IT professionals are never going to call you from computer and software companies like Apple, Microsoft, Norton, and McAfee. If you have a legitimate problem with your computer or software, you have to pick up the phone and call them for help.

🔒 Keep your computer's antivirus software, firewalls, and pop-up blockers up to date.

🔒 Never call a phone number that's included in a pop-up advertisement on your computer screen. Cybercriminals spend millions of dollars purchasing pop-up ads through Google and other search engines.

🔒 Never call computer-repair companies that you find through Google and other search engines. I would recommend only calling well-known companies like McAfee and Norton directly for service issues. If you're close enough to an Apple Store or other computer retailer, I believe it's safer to have the repairs done in person than over the Internet.

🔒 If you receive a call from someone offering you a refund on an antivirus software subscription, hang up the phone. How many companies do you know that actually call you to give money back? Do not, under any circumstances, provide them with a credit card number or bank account and routing numbers. It's a scam, and they're going to steal your money.

🔒 If you're the victim of computer tech fraud, make sure you report the incident to law enforcement. It's the only way we're going to stop this type of crime.

CHAPTER 18

Keeping Kids Safe

I WITNESSED A LOT OF BAD THINGS THROUGHOUT MY LONG career, such as people losing their life savings and small businesses having to close their doors after they were victimized by cybercriminals. What could possibly be worse? That's easy: When the bad guys harm children and steal their innocence. We have the resources to hunt these terrible people down and send them to jail for a very long time, but we can never return a child's innocence.

Today, almost every young child has access to a computer, game console, tablet, or smartphone that's connected to the Internet. Being so connected has changed the way kids interact with the world. Most adults have a difficult time keeping up with their own personal cyber-security, let alone ensuring their children are safe. That's why, over the past several years, we've seen a dramatic increase in cyber-dangers targeting children, including cyberbullying, exposure to taboo mate-rial, online predators, and revealing too much personal information and inappropriate photos on social media. Plus, they have access to the dark web, where drugs, weapons, and anything else is available for sale to anyone who gains access.

While investigating the disappearance of a juvenile in May 1993, special agents from the FBI's Baltimore Division and police detec-tives from Prince George's County, Maryland, identified two suspects who had sexually exploited several juveniles during a twenty-five-year period. Investigators determined that the adults were routinely using computers to transmit sexually explicit images to minors and, in some instances, luring kids into engaging in illicit sexual activity. Further investigations and discussions with experts, in both the FBI and private sector, revealed that computer telecommunications was rapidly becoming one of the most prevalent techniques used by sex offenders to not only share pornographic images of minors, but also to identify and recruit children into sexual relationships. In 1995, based on informa-tion developed during this investigation, the Innocent Images National Initiative (IINI) was created to address the illicit activities conducted by users of commercial and private online services and the Internet.

A few months after reporting to the FBI's field office in Syracuse, New York, I participated in my first IINI investigation in the fall of 1995. During the investigation in Baltimore, investigators examined the subjects' computers and discovered they were trading images of child pornography with individuals across the country. The Baltimore investigation revealed that three hundred and fifty individuals were using the Internet to trade images and communicate, which was a shock to many people in law enforcement. One of the individuals identified during the investigation lived in the Syracuse area, and we had enough probable cause to obtain a warrant to search his residence. Our suspect was a medical professional with a wife and two teenaged children. When questioned, he denied ever looking at these types of images and communicating with other bad guys, but a forensic review of his computer told a completely different story—he had thousands of images of children stored on his computer. He later changed his story and admitted he did look at the photos, but only for a medical research project. He said he kept the project a secret from his office and wife. He eventually pleaded guilty to felony charges and helped us track down other criminals.

Not too long ago, child pornography was difficult to obtain in the U.S. because the risks were too great. The U.S. Postal Inspection Service and FBI did a tremendous job of identifying suspects and apprehending them. These well-publicized sting operations greatly reduced the abhorrent activity—until the Internet came long. The illegal activities started on online bulletin boards and then moved into chat rooms on AOL and Internet Relay Chat, where these monsters found other like-minded predators with whom to communicate and trade. When the Internet really became popular during the 1990s, we started seeing a major increase in the number of online predators. For agents working these kinds of cases, it was like shooting fish in a barrel. I worked dozens of these cases while I was assigned to Syracuse. It was dark and dirty world, and I'm not going to go into detail about the images floating around the web. They would make you sick and give you nightmares.

When I was transferred to Nashville, Tennessee, and promoted to supervisory special agent of the FBI's cybercrime squad there, I gave my first presentation about online safety to a group of inner-city kids between the ages of eight and twelve. My real estate broker's husband mentored many of the kids, and she asked if I would speak to them about cybersecurity. It was the first time I'd talked to a group of kids in quite a while, and I don't think I realized how accessible computers were to them in 2007. When I walked into the room, I scanned the audience and thought most of them were probably too young to have access to the Internet. I figured I'd better come up with some entertaining stories about bank robberies and fugitives. But then I asked the kids how many of them had searched the Internet. About two-thirds of the audience raised its hand. Then I asked how many of them had MySpace accounts, which was the most popular social media at the time. Almost all of them raised their hands. I jokingly asked the kids how they had access to a MySpace account, because you were supposed to be thirteen or older. They laughed at me. Their answers to my next question surprised me. When I asked how many of them knew more about computers than their parents, about half of them raised their hands.

After doing dozens of cybersecurity presentations to children over the past several years, I have become convinced that most parents are happy to have their children at home on computers instead of running around on the streets. As I gave more and more presentations to the community, I noticed a trend: Most kids believe they know more about computers and the Internet than their parents. And what's even scarier is that most of their parents don't even know what they're doing on the Internet. In 2007, our advice to parents was to keep a computer in public places in the house so they could walk by and see what their kids were doing. Under no circumstances, we said, should a child be allowed to have unsupervised use of a computer in his or her bedroom. It was pretty good advice for a few years—until laptops became more afford-able and game consoles and smartphones allowed kids to connect to the web from almost anywhere.

From 2007 until 2011, I supervised the Innocent Images Task Force for the FBI's Memphis Division, which included the area from Memphis to Nashville. We had three full-time FBI special agents and about a dozen full-time task-force officers assigned to the work. The task-force offi-cers were personnel from state and local agencies who were deputized by the U.S. Marshals Service and had the same legal authority as the FBI to investigate federal cases. This program helped the FBI tremendously, as our mission to combat online child predators was only as good as our working relationship with other federal, state, and local law enforcement agencies. During the years in which I ran the task force, we had so many cases that we were only able to investigate the worst of the worst. One year, my team did an especially outstanding job and arrested and prosecuted nearly thirty child predators. The subjects came from all walks of life, including attorneys, pilots, social workers, police officers, doctors, truck drivers, and clergymen. A lot of these bad guys were trading illicit photos and some of them were hurting kids. As effective as we were that year, though, I remember when a former FBI director acknowledged how big the problem really was. He said we couldn't have made a dent in the crisis with even eleven thousand special agents assigned to these types of crimes. But we didn't have eleven thousand agents; in fact, we didn't even have *eleven*.

After working these types of horrific cases, I made a mission of educating parents about the dangers of child exploitation on the Internet. My message wasn't always well received, however, and sometimes I was even told I was being an alarmist. But I was simply presenting the truth from where I sat as an FBI agent. At times, I became extremely frustrated. I'd talk to an elementary school principal about educating her teachers, and she'd tell me her teachers didn't have time and she couldn't force them to sit through my training. Sometimes, the principal would suggest that I contact a parent/teachers' association. I quickly learned, though, that those kinds of groups are more concerned about fundraising and supporting teachers' needs. It infuriated me that schools were teaching children how to use computers and the Internet, but they didn't think it was important to teach them about the dangers. One of my former agents made the best analogy I've heard about what it's like to let your kids have unrestricted access to the Internet. He said, "You're better off giving your kids the keys to your car, a gas card, and a case of beer, and pointing their GPS toward Bourbon Street in New Orleans."

I did make many presentations to parents, and I would provide them with actual case studies and go into painstaking detail explaining how child predators befriend children on the Internet and spend weeks, if not months and years, grooming their victims. The bad guys build rapport with kids and often pretend to be children themselves. They'll find common interests and hobbies with children and befriend them. Eventually, the predators introduce pornographic images to the kids, which is done to trick the children into thinking these kinds of photos are normal. Then they introduce photos of adults engaged in sexual activity with children and try to persuade the children to send nude photos of themselves. The ultimate goal, of course, is to actually meet the child for sexual contact. I know it's terrifying to think about, but there's sadly no shortage of adult men who want to engage in sexual activity with underage boys and girls.

As horrifying as it sounds, I felt it was important to share this warning with parents. Our task force found these monsters in chat rooms, where our officers would pretend to be underage boys and girls. They'd spend hours online with child predators, and, once they sent us pornographic images of children, we tried to set up face-to-face meetings with them. As soon as they exchanged illicit images of kids, it was a federal crime. We wanted to get them off the streets so they wouldn't hurt any more children. The predators almost always took the bait and arranged to meet us. I recall one occasion when the bad guy we arrested had a duffel bag with him. Inside the duffel bag were a stun gun, handcuffs, lubrication, and sexual devices. Being a father of two children, it was absolutely terrifying to investigate these crimes.

During my presentations with parents, I always asked, "Is it important for your children to understand the difference between *real* friends and *virtual* friends?" Almost every parent agreed that it was a very important distinction to make. Then I asked the parents how many friends they had on Facebook. When I asked the parents if they had five hundred, nearly every hand in the room went up. It would go from five hundred to a thousand to one thousand five hundred friends. One parent jumped up and said, "I have two thousand friends!" It appears there are a lot of *adults* who can't tell the difference between real friends and Facebook friends; if a parent can't tell the difference, how are we supposed to teach our children?

Our kids have near-limitless opportunities to interact with virtual friends on platforms their parents have probably never heard of. When my own children were in kindergarten, I explained that the Internet is fun and a great tool for learning, but that there are dangerous places and people on the Internet who would like to hurt them. Whenever I said that in a presentation, though, there was always a mother in the audience who would object. She'd say, "I don't want to scare my children by telling them about all the bad things in the world." Then I would have to explain that refusing to at least make them aware of the threats put her kids at much greater risk.

Having your children understand basic threats on the Internet is a critical first step. As a parent, the day you provide your child with an Internet-connected device, whether it's a computer, tablet, or smartphone, you need to have a serious talk with them. You need to realize that, when your child gets online, he or she has access to excessive violence, hate speech, risky or illegal behaviors, and pornography. You can find any of the first three on YouTube in only a few minutes, and pornography is so readily available on the web now that your kids are going find it no matter how old they are. You can invest money in blocking software like Internet filters and pornography restrictors, but children are smart enough to find ways around it—or they'll just go to a friend's house.

Talking to your kids about the difference between right and wrong is the most important step. If your child comes across something offensive and they come to you, then you have probably succeeded as a parent. Make sure you listen attentively and try not to judge them too quickly. Tell them it's not their fault and ask questions. One day, when my son was about nine years old, he said he wanted to talk to me. Instantly, I recognized that something was wrong. He wasn't immediately forthcoming, but he eventually admitted that he'd seen something on the Internet that was inappropriate. We talked about it, and I assured him that it wasn't his fault. I was relieved he trusted me enough to talk about it, and then I explained the dangers of the Internet to him once again.

I recently gave a cybersecurity presentation to a group of parents of middle school students at an exclusive private school. There was one mother who was shocked by what I was telling her, and she finally asked me, "So, you're saying that I'm a bad parent if I don't know who my daughter is talking to on the Internet?"

I replied, "Of course not. It's impossible to monitor our children twenty-four hours a day. However, if your daughter meets someone on the Internet, and she's never met that person before, and then they decide to meet at the mall and you don't know anything about it, *then* you're a bad parent." I explained the best course of action was to sit down with your kids and have a serious discussion about the dangers of the Internet.

I could write an entire book on Internet safety for our children, and every parent should make it a point to access the National Center for Missing and Exploited Children's website, www.netsmartz.org, which offers great resources, presentations, and games for kids to learn about online safety. Our kids must realize that there are bad guys on the Internet and they should never provide identifying information to people they don't know. They must know the difference between real friends and virtual friends, and we as parents must be aware of what our kids are doing online. Most importantly, you must provide a home environment in which your kids can come to you with questions and concerns. Listen to them without judgment. It's the only way we're going to keep our children safe.

HOW TO AVOID BECOMING A VICTIM

🔒 Parents must understand that there are no rules on the Internet, and that your children can be exposed to pornography, inappropriate material, and hate speech. Keep this in mind when making the decision about giving them access.

🔒 Always be aware of what your children are doing online, including what they're searching for and which websites they're visiting. Install content filters if necessary to be extra safe.

🔒 Realize that there is no shortage of people on the Internet who are looking to harm children.

🔒 Make sure your children understand the difference between real friends and virtual friends.

🔒 If your children have their own social media accounts, their usernames should never be their actual first and last names. That information is too easy to find on Google and other search engines, making it easy for online predators to find them.

🔒 Children should be educated about never providing their name, address, date of birth, or telephone numbers to anyone on the Internet.

🔒 Children should never send photographs of themselves to strangers they meet online.

🔒 Teach your children that anything they write and post on the Internet, including tweets, comments, photographs, and videos, is probably going to stay online forever.

🔒 Set house rules and limit your children's time on computers and other devices. Talk about rules and the consequences of breaking them.

🔒 Teach your children not to open email from strangers, not to respond to hurtful or disturbing messages, and not to arrange face-to-face meetings with anyone they meet online.

🔒 Make sure your children know they can come to you about questions and concerns about material they see on the Internet.

AFTERWORD

WHEN I DECIDED TO WRITE THIS BOOK, MY PURPOSE WAS TO record my stories of fighting cybercrime while working with the Federal Bureau of Investigation and to share everything I learned during those investigations to prevent the average person from becoming the next victim. I can't say enough how upsetting it was to see people's lives being ruined, companies going out of business, senior citizens being ripped off, and our children being hurt when it all could have been prevented. But prevention isn't really going out and developing a new technology to solve the problems. I honestly believe it comes through good, old-fashioned education and awareness.

I feel like there are so many other subjects that I could have written about in this book, and I worry that someone will say, "Hey, you didn't talk about the correct way to set up my home network," or, "What I should do with my router?" or, "What kind of security suite should I purchase to protect my information?" There is so much information out there about those subjects and so many varying opinions. Understand that this book wasn't written to teach you how to secure your computer and network; my goal was more about teaching you how to avoid becoming the next cybercrime victim.

Where is the future of cybercrime headed? That's a scary question. In 2018, there were about eighty-seven million people around the world using Facebook, and many of them were sharing too much of their personal information with strangers. One of the biggest issues with social media is privacy, so ask yourself what Facebook is doing to protect us. In July 2018, Facebook was hit with the maximum financial penalty allowed under British law for failing to safeguard its user data and for not informing tens of millions of its users that the political data firm Cambridge Analytica harvested their information for use in political campaigns. And, of course, Facebook was already facing intense scrutiny for allowing a Russian operation with ties to the Kremlin to purchase thousands of advertisements on its platform to influence the 2016 U.S. presidential election.

I always ask people in my cybercrime presentations, "How many people are upset about what happened with Facebook?" A lot of people in the audience raise their hands, but then I remind them that they willingly gave their most personal information—their name, date of birth, hometown, and family photos—to this social media platform. We'll even share photos and videos, and we'll inform strangers when we're not home or on vacation and traveling out of the country. We have to take better steps to safeguard our privacy, so ask yourself if you're sharing too much personal information on social media.

Right now, nearly every one of us owns a smartphone and has access to the Internet at our fingertips. In most instances, it's not our smartphones that are insecure and vulnerable to cybercriminals; it's the millions of apps we're downloading onto our phones and other devices. Be careful with the apps you're downloading to your machines. On your phone and tablet, make sure you're downloading and installing legitimate apps only from Apple's App Store and the Google Play Store.

Another important topic we didn't cover in this book is what's called the *Internet of things* (IOT), which is made up of all the devices we're using that connect to the Internet. We're filling our homes with thermostats, garage-door openers, refrigerators, light bulbs, and security cameras that have a direct line to the web! You can walk down the aisles at Best Buy and see hundreds of devices that were introduced to make our lives easier and more convenient, but, at the same time, a lot of these devices have default and insecure passwords. We can control many of them through apps on our phones. What happens if you're using the same username and password for your home security system that you are for your Yahoo! email? If Yahoo! has another data breach, the bad guys are going to be able to gain access to the security cameras inside your house. Imagine what they'll be able to watch from thousands of miles away! Remember that we need to use different passwords and two-factor authentication with these devices, as well.

What about the next generation of so-called *smart assistants*? I recently watched a video showing the Google Assistant calling a restaurant and making a reservation for dinner—all without any human assistance. The computer, all by itself, dialed the number, greeted the person who answered, and engaged in a complex back-and-forth discussion with the hostess at a Chinese restaurant. It was able to answer questions, change direction, fill silence, and even use human triggers like "hmm" and "ah, okay" to disguise the fact that it was, in fact, a machine. We're already using Google Assistant and Apple's Siri to dial the phone, pull up sports scores, and provide us with directions or restaurant recommendations. But it's scary to think that one day, virtual assistants will be used to call us, and we'll believe the human-like voice on the other end is actually our doctor, lawyer, or banker. I fear that companies are going to jump into this technology to save money and reduce their overhead without completely understanding the risks involved. It's only a matter of time before the bad guys figure out a million ways to use this and other new technologies to illicitly gain access to our personal information.

And then there are the growing fields of blockchain and cryptocurrency. I've heard so much discussion recently about blockchain, which is the technology at the heart of bitcoin and other virtual currencies. Blockchain is essentially a database that is shared across a network of computers; the *Harvard Business Review* describes it as an "open, distributed ledger that can record transactions between two parties efficiently and in a verifiable and permanent way. The ledger itself can also be programmed to trigger transactions automatically." Each party on a blockchain has access to the entire database and its complete history. No single person or entity controls the data or the information, and, once a transaction is entered into the database and accounts are entered, the records can't be altered because they're linked to every other transaction that occurred before them. Users are given a unique thirty-plus-character alphanumeric address that identifies them or they can remain anonymous. I recently participated in a panel about blockchain, and everyone is talking about how it is the new technology for information security. However, based on the discussions I've had,

I can't understand how blockchain would have prevented *any* of the crimes we've discussed in this book. I'm sure there are many practical applications for blockchain, and I've noticed that a lot of companies and organizations are exploring blockchain as information security solutions. But, when they're not yet implementing the basics and fundamentals of cybersecurity, blockchain isn't going to change anything.

I'm gravely concerned about the growing market for bitcoin and other cryptocurrency. Now there are even ICOs, which are *Internet coin offerings*. People are investing a lot of money in bitcoin and other cryptocurrency, and businesses are starting to jump on the bandwagon too. I heard a presenter talking about bitcoin and cryptocurrency, and I couldn't help but snicker while listening to him. The moderator asked me why I was laughing, and I said, "Look, my only experience with cryptocurrency was with cybercrime victims who had to use it to pay a ransom to have their personal information unlocked."

Cybercrime groups are already targeting cryptocurrency. The infamous North Korean cybercrime ring Lazarus has been targeting cryptocurrency exchanges, fintech (*financial technology*) companies, and banks with a malware campaign called AppleJeus, and they're not alone in trying to break into these exchanges. Are there legitimate purposes for cryptocurrency? I'm sure there might be some out there, but I've only seen it used by cybercriminals.

In conclusion, I have to say that I was very, very humbled to work with the FBI for twenty-nine years. I know there has been a lot of controversy associated with the FBI over the years, but I was extremely proud to work for such a tremendous organization. I'm also honored to have been able to share my experiences with you. Hopefully what you learned will help prevent you from becoming the next cybercrime victim.

RESOURCES TO PREVENT CYBERCRIME

AARP Foundation ElderWatch
www.aarpelderwatch.org

Better Business Bureau
www.bbb.org/scam-stopper

Common Sense Media
https://www.commonsensemedia.org/

ConnectSafely.org
https://www.connectsafely.org

Consumer Financial Protection Bureau
www.consumerfinance.gov

Department of Homeland Security
https://www.dhs.gov/stopthinkconnect

Federal Bureau of Investigation
https://www.fbi.gov/investigate/cyber

Federal Trade Commission (FTC)
www.consumer.gov

Financial Industry Regulatory Authority (FINRA)
www.finra.org/complaint

Internet Crime Complaint Center (IC3)
https://www.ic3.gov/default.aspx

Internet Safety 101
https://internetsafety101.org

National Center for Missing & Exploited Children
https://www.netsmartz.org/

National Council on Aging (NCOA)
https://www.ncoa.org/public-policy-action/elder-justice

Phishing.org
http://www.phishing.org/10-ways-to-avoid-phishing-scams

Romance Scams: Scam Busters and Dating Site Reviews
https://www.romancescams.org

Stop.Think.Connect.
https://www.stopthinkconnect.org

Two-Factor Authentication (2FA)
https://twofactorauth.org

U.S. Postal Service Office of Inspector General
www.uspsoig.gov

WORKS CITED

"159 Arrests and 766 Money Mules Identified in Global Action Week Against Money Muling." *Europol.* November 28, 2017. Accessed July 5, 2018. https://www.europol.europa.eu/newsroom/news/159-arrests-and-766-money-mules-identified-in-global-action-week-against-money-muling.

"2017 Cybercrime Report." Herjavec Group. October 18, 2017. Accessed July 7, 2018. https://www.herjavecgroup.com/cybercrime-report-2017.

"2017 Internet Crime Report." Federal Bureau of Investigation. Accessed July 8, 2018. https://www.fbi.gov/news/stories/2017-internet-crime-report-released-050718.

"Banking Tips for Small Businesses." FDIC *Consumer News.* Winter 2011/2012. Accessed July 27, 2018. https://www.fdic.gov/consumers/consumer/news/cnwin1112/win1112bw.pdf.

"Commercial Banks in the U.S." Federal Reserve Bank of St. Louis. Accessed June 30, 2018. https://fred.stlouisfed.org/series/USNUM.

"Cybercriminals Utilize Social Engineering Techniques to Obtain Employee Credentials to Conduct Payroll Diversion." Federal Bureau of Investigation. Accessed August 13, 2018. http://image.communications.cyber.nj.gov/lib/fe3e15707564047c7c1270/m/1/b2e366a7-1abf-4352-aa8f-ec3236c1935d.pdf.

"Dating & romance." Australian Competition & Consumer Commission. Accessed August 21, 2018. https://www.scamwatch.gov.au/types-of-scams/dating-romance.

"Email Statistics Report, 2018–2022." The Radicati Group, Inc. Accessed June 28, 2018. https://www.radicati.com/wp/wp-content/uploads/2018/01/Email_Statistics_Report,_2018-2022_Executive_Summary.pdf.

"FBI: Email Account Compromise Losses Reach $12B," *Dark Reading.* July 13, 2018. Accessed July 15, 2018. https://www.darkreading.com/threat-intelligence/fbi-email-account-compromise-losses-reach-$12b-/d/d-id/1332294.

"FBI Warns of Rise in Schemes Targeting Businesses and Online Fraud of Financial Officers and Individuals." Federal Bureau of Investigation. March 29, 2016. Accessed July 22, 2018. https://www.fbi.gov/contact-us/field-offices/cleveland/news/press-releases/fbi-warns-of-rise-in-schemes-targeting-businesses-and-online-fraud-of-financial-officers-and-individuals.

"Ghanaian Man Pleads Guilty To His Role In Internet Fraud Scheme." United State's Attorney's Office Western District of New York. Accessed August 13, 2018. https://www.justice.gov/usao-wdny/pr/ghanaian-man-pleads-guilty-his-role-internet-romance-fraud-scheme.

"Home Depot To Pay Millions For Data Breach." *Fortune.* March 8, 2016. Accessed July 19, 2018. http://fortune.com/2016/03/08/home-depot-data-breach-2.

"International Business E-Mail Compromise Takedown." Federal Bureau of Investigation. June 11, 2018. Accessed June 12, 2018. https://www.fbi.gov/news/stories/international-bec-takedown-061118.

"ISTR 23: Insights into the Cyber Security Threat Landscape." Symantec. March 21, 2018. Accessed June 9, 2018. https://www.symantec.com/blogs/threat-intelligence/istr-23-cyber-security-threat-landscape.

"Mobile data report: Focus on phishing." Wandera. July 2017. Accessed June 19, 2018. https://www.wandera.com/wandera-mobile-data-report.

"Mobile Fact Sheet." Pew Research Center. February 5, 2018. Accessed May 31, 2018. http://www.pewinternet.org/fact-sheet/mobile.

"Online Financial Cybercrime Victims Struggle to Recover All Their Lost Money." Kaspersky Lab. January 25, 2017. Accessed June 19, 2018. https://www.kaspersky.com/about/press-releases/2017_online-financial-cybercrime-victims-struggle-to-recover-all-their-lost-money.

"Owners of Tech Support Scams in South Florida and Costa Rica Charged with Federal Fraud Offenses." United States Attorney's Office Southern District of Illinois. Accessed August 13, 2018. https://www.justice.gov/usao-sdil/pr/owners-tech-support-scams-south-florida-and-costa-rica-charged-federal-fraud-offenses.

"Romance Scams: Online Imposters Break Hearts and Bank Accounts." Federal Bureau of Investigation. February 13, 2017. Accessed August 21, 2018. https://www.fbi.gov/news/stories/romance-scams.

"Russian Citizen who Helped Develop the 'Citadel' Malware Toolkit is Sentenced." United States Attorney's Office Northern District of Georgia. July 19, 2017. Accessed July 28, 2018. https://www.justice.gov/usao-ndga/pr/russian-citizen-who-helped-develop-citadel-malware-toolkit-sentenced-0.

"Scammers phish for mortgage closing costs." Federal Trade Commission. March 18, 2016. Accessed July 14, 2018. https://www.consumer.ftc.gov/blog/scammers-phish-mortgage-closing-costs.

"The Human Factor 2018 Report: People Centered Threats Define The Landscape." Proofpoint. Accessed July 12, 2018. https://www.proofpoint.com/us/human-factor-2018.

"The Little Book of Big Scams, Fourth Edition." Metropolitan Police and New Scotland Yard. Accessed July 7, 2018. https://www.ourwatch.org.uk/wp-content/uploads/2018/06/the-little-book-of-big-scams.pdf.

"Up to $200 Billion in Illegal Cybercrime Profits Is Laundered Each Year, Comprehensive Research Study Reveals." *CNBC*. March 16, 2018. Accessed July 2, 2018. https://www.cnbc.com/2018/03/16/globe-newswire-up-to-200-billion-in-illegal-cybercrime-profits-is-laundered-each-year-comprehensive-research-study-reveals.html.

Baig, Edward. "Outsiders may be reading your Gmail: Here's how to stop them." *USA Today*. July 3, 2018. Accessed August 9, 2018. https://www.usatoday.com/story/tech/talkingtech/2018/07/03/gmail-how-stop-outsiders-reading-your-inbox/755298002.

Brewster, Thomas. "Five Arrested As Cops Hunt Two Of The Biggest Ransomware Strains Ever." *Forbes*. December 20, 2017. Accessed May 26, 2018. https://www.forbes.com/sites/thomasbrewster/2017/12/20/ransomware-arrests-for-cerber-and-ctb-locker/#4193fcc315a9.

Dimon, Laura and Graham Rayman. "State Supreme Court judge loses over $1M in real estate scam." *New York Daily News*. June 20, 2017. Accessed July 19, 2018. http://www.nydailynews.com/new-york/state-supreme-court-judge-loses-1m-real-estate-email-scam-article-1.3263091?cid=bitly.

Enge, Eric. "Mobile vs Desktop Usage in 2018: Mobile takes the lead." *Stone Temple*. April 27, 2018. Accessed July 2, 2018. https://www.stonetemple.com/mobile-vs-desktop-usage-study.

Evans, Martin. "Fraud and cyber crime are now the country's most common offences." *The Telegraph.* January 19, 2017. Accessed June 8, 2018. https://www.telegraph.co.uk/news/2017/01/19/fraud-cyber-crime-now-countrys-common-offences.

Furst, Randy. "'Money Mule' charged with scamming 3 Minnesotans out of $360,000." *Star Tribune.* January 10, 2018. Accessed July 27, 2018. http://www.startribune.com/commerce-dept-money-mule-charged-with-ripping-off-3-minnesotans-of-360-000/468666463.

Hackett, Robert. "LinkedIn Lost 167 Million Account Credentials in Data Breach." *Fortune.* May 18, 2016. Accessed July 2, 2018. http://fortune.com/2016/05/18/linkedin-data-breach-email-password.

Hamilton, Isobel Asher. "A 'Game of Thrones' thief and dam hacker: These are the FBI's 41 most-wanted cyber criminals." *Business Insider.* July 22, 2018. Accessed August 13, 2018. https://www.businessinsider.com/these-are-the-fbis-41-most-wanted-cyber-criminals-2018-6?r=UK&IR=T.

Iansiti, Marco and Karim R. Lakhani. "The Truth About Blockchain." *Harvard Business Review.* January–February 2017 issue. Accessed August 23, 2018. https://hbr.org/2017/01/the-truth-about-blockchain.

Isaac, Mike, Katie Benner, and Sheera Frenkel. "Uber Hid 2016 Breach, Paying Hackers to Delete Stolen Data." *New York Times.* November 21, 2017. Accessed June 18, 2018. https://www.nytimes.com/2017/11/21/technology/uber-hack.html.

Johnson, Alex. "Massive Phishing Attack Targets Gmail Users." *NBC News.* May 3, 2017. Accessed June 11, 2018. https://www.nbcnews.com/tech/security/massive-phishing-attack-targets-millions-gmail-users-n754501.

Johnson, Bobbie. "Sarah Palin vs the hacker," *The Telegraph.* May 27, 2010. Accessed July 1, 2018. https://www.telegraph.co.uk/news/worldnews/sarah-palin/7750050/Sarah-Palin-vs-the-hacker.html.

Kanter, Jake. "An FBI agent mapped out the countries capable of unleashing a crippling cyberattack on the US." *Business Insider.* June 4, 2018. Accessed June 19, 2018. https://www.businessinsider.com/fbi-aristedes-mahairas-these-4-nations-pose-biggest-cyber-risk-to-us-2018-6.

McCoy, Kevin. "Target to Pay $18.5M for 2013 data breach that affected 41 million consumers." *USA Today.* May 23, 2017. Accessed June 8, 2018. https://www.usatoday.com/story/money/2017/05/23/target-pay-185m-2013-data-breach-affected-consumers/102063932.

Morgan, Steve. "Top 5 cybersecurity facts, figures and statistics for 2018." *Cybersecurity Business Report.* January 23, 2018. Accessed June 30, 2018. https://www.csoonline.com/article/3153707/security/top-5-cybersecurity-facts-figures-and-statistics.html.

Mullin, Gemma and Emma Lake. "Malicious Virus: What is WannaCry ransomware? Malware used to cripple NHS in 2017 cyberattack." *The Sun.* March 29, 2018. Accessed May 30, 2018. https://www.thesun.co.uk/tech/3562470/wannacry-ransomware-nhs-cyberattack-hackers-virus.

Nair, Sharmila. "SamSam ransomware victims lose RM23.9 mil to attackers." *The Star Online.* August 2, 2018. Accessed August 10, 2018. https://www.thestar.com.my/tech/tech-news/2018/08/02/samsam-ransomware-victims-lose-rm239mil-to-the-attackers.

Ng, Alfred. "South Korean web host pays largest ransomware demand ever." *Cnet.* June 20, 2017. Accessed August 12, 2018. https://www.cnet.com/news/largest-ransomware-ever-demand-south-korea-web-host.

O'Sullivan, Donie. "Facebook broke the law and faces maximum fine for Cambridge Analytica scandal, UK watchdog says." *CNN.* July 11, 2018. Accessed July 29, 2018. https://money.cnn.com/2018/07/10/technology/facebook-britain-ico-cambridge-analytica-fine/index.html.

Rankin, Bert. "A Brief History of Malware—Its Evolution and Impact." *Lastline.* April 5, 2018. Accessed June 3, 2018. https://www.lastline.com/blog/history-of-malware-its-evolution-and-impact.

Rodriguez, Joe Fitzgerald. "Alleged Muni 'hacker' demands $73,000 ransom, some computers in stations restored." *San Francisco Examiner.* November 27, 2016. Accessed July 1, 2018. http://www.sfexaminer.com/alleged-muni-hacker-demands-73000-ransom-computers-stations-restored.

Ropeik, Annie. "Small Indiana Nonprofit Falls Victim To Ransom Cyberattack." *NPR.* May 20, 2017. Accessed July 13, 2018. https://www.npr.org/2017/05/20/529257365/small-indiana-nonprofit-falls-victim-to-ransom-cyberattack.

Rosenblatt, Seth. "Cybercriminals' money-laundering backbone: Cash-strapped consumers." *The Parallax.* December 14, 2016. Accessed July 27, 2018. https://www.the-parallax.com/2016/12/14/cybercriminals-money-muling-consumers.

Schwartz, Mathew J. "FBI: Global Business Email Compromise Losses Hit $12.5 Billion." *Bank Info Security.* July 16, 2018. Accessed August 1, 2018. https://www.bankinfosecurity.com/fbi-alert-reported-ceo-fraud-losses-hit-125-billion-a-11206.

Specht, Bettina. "Email Client Market Share Trends for the First Half of 2018." *Litmus Software.* July 13, 2018. Accessed June 27, 2018. https://litmus.com/blog/email-client-market-share-trends-first-half-of-2018.

Stamos, Alex. "Preparing for the future of security requires focusing on defense and diversity." Facebook Security. July 26, 2017. Accessed June 1, 2018. https://www.facebook.com/notes/facebook-security/preparing-for-the-future-of-security-requires-focusing-on-defense-and-diversity/10154629522900766.

Strauss, Steve. "Cyber threat is huge for small businesses." *USA Today.* October 20, 2017. Accessed June 1, 2018. https://www.usatoday.com/story/money/columnist/strauss/2017/10/20/cyber-threat-huge-small-businesses/782716001.

Swanson, Brena. "Washington D.C. couple loses $1.5 million in mortgage closing cost phishing scam." *Housing Wire.* August 11, 2017. Accessed July 19, 2018. https://www.housingwire.com/articles/40979-video-washington-dc-couple-loses-15-million-in-mortgage-closing-cost-phishing-scam.

Wescott, Ben. "International cyber crime ring smashed after more than $530 million stolen." *CNN.* February 8, 2018. Accessed July 19, 2018. https://www.cnn.com/2018/02/08/world/us-cyber-crime-ring-arrests-intl/index.html.

Wilson, John. "Real Estate Email Scams—Don't Get Tricked!" Agari. June 29, 2017. Accessed July 19, 2018. https://www.agari.com/identity-intelligence-blog/real-estate-email-scams.

Winton, Richard. "Hollywood hospital pays $17,000 in bitcoin to hackers; FBI investigating." *Los Angeles Times.* February 18, 2016. Accessed July 1, 2018. http://www.latimes.com/business/technology/la-me-ln-hollywood-hospital-bitcoin-20160217-story.html.

Wright, Lori. "New survey explores the changing landscape of teamwork." Microsoft. April 19, 2018. Accessed July 29, 2018. https://www.microsoft.com/en-us/microsoft-365/blog/2018/04/19/new-survey-explores-the-changing-landscape-of-teamwork.

York, Alex. "61 Social Media Statistics to Bookmark for 2018." *Sprout Social.* Accessed June 13, 2018. https://sproutsocial.com/insights/social-media-statistics.